Assess for
Success

Second Edition

Assess for

Success

Second Edition

A Practitioner's Handbook on
Transition Assessment

Patricia L. Sitlington

Debra A. Neubert • *Wynne H. Begun*

Richard C. Lombard • *Pamela J. Leconte*

Education Resource Center
University of Delaware
Newark, DE 19716-2940
A Joint Publication

DCDT

Division on Career
Development and Transition

CORWIN PRESS
A SAGE Publications Company
Thousand Oaks, CA 91320

T 52940

For information:

Corwin Press
A SAGE Publications Company
2455 Teller Road
Thousand Oaks, California 91320
www.corwinpress.com

SAGE Publications Ltd.
1 Oliver's Yard
55 City Road
London EC1Y 1SP
United Kingdom

SAGE Publications India Pvt. Ltd.
B 1/I 1 Mohan Cooperative
    Industrial Area
Mathura Road, New Delhi 110 044
India

SAGE Publications Asia-Pacific Pte. Ltd.
33 Pekin Street #02-01
Far East Square
Singapore 048763

Printed in the United States of America

Library of Congress Cataloging-in-Publication Data

Assess for success: A practicioner's handbook on transition assessment/Patricia L. Sitlington, Debra A. Neubert, Wynne H. Begun, Rick Lombard, and Pamela Leconte—2nd ed.
     p. cm.
Previously published: Reston, Va.: Council for Exceptional Children, [1996].
Includes bibliographical references and index.
ISBN-13: 978-1-4129-5280-4 (cloth: alk. paper)
ISBN-13: 978-1-4129-5281-1 (pbk.: alk. paper)
   1. Youth with disabilities—Services for—United States. 2. Students with disabilities—Services for—United States. 3. People with disabilities—Vocational guidance—United States. 4. School-to-work transition—United States. 5. Social integration—United States. 6. Needs assessment—United States. I. Sitlington, Patricia L. II. Neubert, Debra A. III. Begun, Wynne H. IV. Title.

HV1569.3.Y68A87 2007
362.4083—dc22   2006102761

This book is printed on acid-free paper.

07   08   09   10   11   10   9   8   7   6   5   4   3   2   1

Acquisitions Editor:	Kathleen McLane
Editorial Assistant:	Mary Dang
Production Editor:	Beth A. Bernstein
Copy Editor:	Halim Dunsky
Typesetter:	C&M Digitals (P) Ltd.
Proofreader:	Tracy Marcynzsyn
Indexer:	John Hulse
Cover Designer:	Monique Hahn

Contents

Preface

The Individuals with Disabilities Education Improvement Act of 2004 (IDEA 2004) directly addresses transition assessment. It also mandates that each student be provided with a Summary of Performance (SOP) before he or she exits the school system. Both of these additions hold tremendous potential for integrating the results of transition assessment into the transition planning process for the student—via the Individualized Education Program (IEP).

Preparing for transition into all aspects of adult life is like taking a long trip. To proceed effectively it helps to have an itinerary, a timetable, and a map. As with any trip, it is important to make frequent progress checks to be sure you are still on the right road and are moving along at the speed you anticipated. Also, frequent progress checks allow for orderly course corrections, side trips, and changes in destination. Transition assessment is an individualized, ongoing process that helps students with disabilities and their families define appropriate personal destinations or goals and check progress along the way.

The vision for life beyond school should begin to be conceived in the elementary and middle school years. IDEA 2004 mandates that by age 16 the IEP must reflect a clear timetable and itinerary for accomplishing specific goals. (We believe that this process should start much earlier—and no later than age 14.) Assessment is crucial in establishing this timetable and in keeping the IEP team on track. However, deciding what to assess and how assessment data will be collected and used can be a challenge.

This is the second edition of this handbook, and we have made a number of changes in this edition. This handbook is designed to be used by everyone on the IEP team, including the student, family members, general and special educators, and adult providers, as they assist a student of any disability and functioning level in defining his or her vision of the future and in reaching this vision. The assessment process described in this handbook builds upon a variety of information emphasizing the use of transition assessment techniques and community-based settings in gathering the information needed for transition planning.

The first chapter provides an overview of the transition assessment process, including its purpose and the laws requiring that transition assessment be carried out. Chapter 2 approaches transition assessment within the context of career development and provides a checklist and set of assessment questions to help teachers pinpoint where along the awareness, exploration, preparation, and assimilation career path a student is functioning.

Chapter 3 presents the role of the student in the transition assessment process and the development of self-determination skills to assist the student in this role. The focus of Chapter 4 is on integrating the results of transition assessment into the IEP. Sample case studies and transition goals are provided. Chapter 5 discusses the role of the individual, family members, special education and general education teachers, support staff, and adult service providers in the assessment process.

Chapter 6 then presents an overview of methods that practitioners can use to collect information about the student's needs, strengths, preferences, and interests throughout the transition planning process. This chapter also presents methods of gathering information about the demands of current and potential future living, working, and educational environments. The final chapter presents a format for making the best match between the demands of these environments and the needs, strengths, preferences, and interests of the student. This chapter also presents questions that need to be asked during the transition process and procedures for developing an assessment plan.

Transition assessment is not a magical process. It is simply assisting students in identifying where they would like to live, work, and learn when they become adults and in determining the supports, accommodations, and preparation they will need in order to reach their goals. We hope that this handbook will help you as you assist students in this process.

Acknowledgments

Our appreciation goes to the individuals with disabilities with whom we have worked and to their family members and the professionals who work with them to make the transition to adult life as smooth as possible. They have shown us how critical the assessment process is in this transition. We also acknowledge the major contributions of those graduate students at the University of Northern Iowa who assisted with editing and coordinating the many components of this handbook. These individuals include Sonya Elzey, Crystal Stokes, and Heather Trilk. Our thanks also go to our colleagues who supported us during the writing of this handbook.

Thanks, too, to the following reviewers of this edition for their suggestions and comments: Gary Clark, Bob Loyd, and Jeanne Repetto. Finally, we extend our appreciation to Kathleen McLane, Mary Dang, Beth Bernstein, and Halim Dunsky for their editorial assistance in getting this handbook into its final form.

About the Authors

Patricia L. Sitlington is Professor and Coordinator of the graduate emphasis in Career/Vocational Programming and Transition at the University of Northern Iowa. She has been a secondary classroom teacher and State Department staff member, as well as program consultant. She has written extensively in the field of transition, and is coauthor of *Transition Education and Services for Students With Disabilities*, a major textbook in the field. Her main research interests include assessment, outcomes studies of young adults with and without disabilities, and cross-disciplinary collaboration.

Debra A. Neubert is Professor in the Department of Special Education at the University of Maryland in College Park. She has taught undergraduate and graduate courses in secondary special education and transition services for the past 20 years and has directed numerous personnel training grants from the U.S. Office of Special Education and Rehabilitation Services. As Principal Investigator of On-Campus Outreach, a federally funded outreach project, she investigated practices and outcomes for students ages 18 to 21 with significant disabilities who receive special education services at postsecondary sites. Her research interests include transition assessment and case management for students with disabilities exiting the school system and access to postsecondary education for students with disabilities.

Wynne H. Begun is Director of Special Education in the Blue Valley School District in Overland Park, Kansas. Wynne earned her doctorate from the University of Kansas. She is a past president of the Division on Career Development and Transition. Wynne has been instrumental in developing innovative, nationally recognized programming in the area of transition throughout her career. She is especially proud of the Blue Valley ACCESS Program that serves students ages 18 to 21.

Richard C. Lombard is Professor of Special Education at University of Wisconsin–Whitewater. He has authored or co-authored more than thirty articles in professional journals with an emphasis on transition assessment, vocational evaluation, community-based transition models, and inclusion. Dr. Lombard served as President of the International Division on Career Development and Transition (DCDT) in 1999-2000. He currently serves as the Sweden Exchange Coordinator for UW-Whitewater and Umea University in Umea, Sweden. His international service includes work in Sweden, Australia, Nepal, India, and Trinidad.

Pamela J. Leconte earned her EdD from George Washington University (GWU) in Washington, DC. She directs the Collaborative Vocational Evaluation Training program at GWU and is Assistant Research Professor. She has worked in community rehabilitation, public schools, and university settings, and has served in leadership roles in a number of national and state professional associations.

1

Overview of Transition Assessment

Transition assessment is an ongoing and coordinated process that begins in the middle school years and continues until students with disabilities graduate or exit the school system. Transition assessment assists students with disabilities and their families to identify and plan for postsecondary goals and adult roles. Adult roles can include independent living, employment, postsecondary education, community involvement, and social/personal relationships. The purpose of this chapter is to

- Describe why transition assessment is important for students with disabilities
- Explain legislation that impacts transition assessment

Adolescents with disabilities and their families face challenges at various transition points, such as moving from middle school to high school, from high school to a postsecondary education program, or from home to living in the community. Each transition point requires a determination of appropriate experiences and services that will assist individuals in selecting and achieving their goals. Due to the diversity of these goals, various professionals, including special and general educators, career and technology educators, counselors, vocational assessment personnel, transition specialists, paraprofessionals, employers, and adult service providers, may participate in transition assessment. However, the success of this process depends on the active involvement of students with disabilities and their families. Transition assessment provides the vehicle for this active involvement and for ongoing transition planning.

Students with disabilities and their families need to understand what types of transition assessment data are most useful at different life junctures, who is in the best position to collect assessment data, and how the results of transition assessment will be used. Students should be actively involved in determining what assessment activities they will participate in (e.g., interest inventories, internships, exploration of support services at colleges). Some students may benefit from person-centered planning approaches in which a group of professionals and family members assist a student to identify vocational, community, and domestic experiences that will allow them to achieve goals in various environments. Most important, students with disabilities need to understand how they can use transition assessment activities to identify their needs, strengths, preferences, and interests as they prepare for adult roles. Students can then use this information to participate actively in Individualized Education Program (IEP) meetings when transition services are discussed.

WHAT IS TRANSITION ASSESSMENT?

Transition assessment provides a foundation for planning students' post-school outcomes and is conceptualized broadly as an ongoing and coordinated process. Methods from career education, vocational assessment and evaluation, career and technology education, vocational rehabilitation, and curriculum-based assessment are used in the process. Transition assessment facilitates individual choice by allowing students with disabilities to

- Identify individual needs, strengths, preferences, interests, and post-school goals
- Identify a course of study in high school to achieve postschool goals
- Identify potential living, working, and educational environments to achieve postschool goals
- Identify programs, services, supports, and resources to achieve postschool goals

In addition, transition assessment data provide secondary educators with valid information to update IEPs and compile a SOP for each student as the student exits school. This facilitates compliance with the Individuals with Disabilities Education Improvement Act of 2004 (IDEA 2004).

Definition and Purposes

We propose the following definition for transition assessment:

Transition assessment is an ongoing process of collecting information on the student's strengths, needs, preferences, and interests as they relate to the demands of current and future living, learning, and working environments. This process should begin in middle school and continue until the student graduates or exits high school. Information from this process should be used to drive the IEP and transition planning process and to develop the SOP document detailing the student's academic and functional performance and postsecondary goals.

In addition, the purposes of transition assessment are to assist students to

- Determine their level of career development so they can participate in appropriate career education activities
- Identify their needs, strengths, interests, and preferences in relation to postschool goals for living, learning, and working
- Identify a focus of study to facilitate the attainment of postschool goals
- Identify self-determination skills needed to participate in general education courses and pursue postschool goals
- Identify accommodations, supports, assistive technology, and/or adult services to attain postschool goals
- Compile the SOP document upon graduation or exit from school

The definition and purposes of transition assessment build on our earlier work (Neubert, 2003; Sitlington, Neubert, Begun, Lombard, & Leconte, 1996; Sitlington & Neubert, 1998) and on a definition of transition assessment endorsed by the Division of Career Development and Transition (Sitlington, Neubert, & Leconte, 1997).

TRANSITION: A LOOK AT WHERE WE'VE BEEN

Since the early 1980s, special education has focused on the need for transition services to assist students with disabilities to plan for the future. Documentation of poor postsecondary outcomes for individuals with disabilities through follow-up studies led to development of secondary and postsecondary transition models, identification of recommended practices, and training of personnel to provide transition services in secondary and postsecondary settings. Legislation in special education and vocational rehabilitation for the past 30 years has shaped current transition assessment practices for secondary students with disabilities.

Will's (1984) early definition of transition, which focused on moving "from school to employment," was broadened to include various postschool outcomes. Halpern's (1994) definition of transition remains timely and is used for the purposes of this book:

Transition refers to a change in status from behaving primarily as a student to assuming emergent roles in the community. These roles include employment, participating in postsecondary education, maintaining a home, becoming actively involved in the community and experiencing satisfactory personal and social relationships. The process of enhancing transition involves the participation and coordination of school programs, adult agency services and natural supports within the community. The foundation for transition should be laid during the elementary and middle school years, guided by the broad concept of career development. Transition planning should begin no later than age 14, and students should be encouraged, to the full extent of their capabilities, to assume a maximum amount of responsibility for such planning. (p. 117)

In 1990, the Individuals with Disabilities Education Act (IDEA) provided a similar definition of transition and mandated that transition services be included in students' IEPs by age 16. In addition, this legislation addressed assessment and self-determination by requiring that the statement of transition services be based on students' needs and interests and that students be invited to IEP meetings when transition services were discussed. These mandates remained in the IDEA Amendments of 1997; however, the age for including transition services in IEPs was changed to 14 and the requirement to identify a student's course of study (e.g., college preparation courses, career and technical courses) was added.

The School to Work Opportunities Act of 1994 (STWOA) also drew attention to the need for transition planning for all youth. Although the STWOA was discontinued in 2001, it continues to provide a foundation for school-based, work-based, and connecting activities in career and technology programs and youth employment programs that mirror the transition services we've come to know in special education.

STWOA and several other key pieces of legislation since that time (e.g., Goals 2000; No Child Left Behind Act of 2001) emphasized the need for educational reform in public school systems. Therefore, the need to align secondary transition services within the reform movement has become a prominent theme. Blending transition services with state standards for academic content areas, state assessments to determine students' adequate yearly progress in reading and math, and greater accountability for ensuring that all students reach higher standards presents challenges and opportunities for educators today. IDEA 2004 reinforces the themes of increased expectations and accountability for students with disabilities by mandating access to general education with appropriate supports, the identification of measurable postschool outcomes for students, and the determination of students' goals and interests/needs through age-appropriate transition assessment. The following section provides more detailed information on the impact of IDEA 2004 on transition assessment.

IDEA 2004

One of the purposes of IDEA 2004 is to ensure that students have a free and appropriate education that emphasizes special education and related services in relation to individual needs and preparation for further education, employment, and independent living opportunities; the term "further education" is a new addition to the IDEA 2004 purpose statement. The term "transition assessment" is addressed directly for the first time under Section 614 (IEP requirements) and the definition of transition services has changed slightly from IDEA 1990 and the 1997 Amendments. It is unfortunate to note that the term "student" has been replaced with "child" throughout the Act. Finally, assistive technology services and devices and universal design are addressed in IDEA 2004; this is relevant in terms of assessing students' needs for assistive technology to participate in regular education, postsecondary education, and community settings. For additional information on the statute (IDEA 2004), readers are referred to http://thomas.loc.gov and http://www.ed.gov/policy/speced/guid/idea/idea2004.html. Information on the Final Regulations for IDEA 2004 issued by the U.S. Department of Education on August 3, 2006, can be found at http://www.wrightslaw.com/idea/law.htm.

Transition Services

Transition services in IDEA 2004 are defined as a coordinated set of activities for a child with a disability that

> . . . is designed to be within a results-oriented process, that is focused on improving the academic and functional achievement of the child with a disability to facilitate the child's movement from school to postschool activities, including postsecondary education; vocational education; integrated employment (including supported employment); continuing and adult education; adult services; independent living or community participation; [602(34)(A)] and Is based on the individual child's needs, taking into account the child's strengths, preferences and interests. [602(34)(B)]

IEP Requirements

There are a number of changes to the IEP process in IDEA 2004. IEPs are to include a statement of measurable annual goals, including academic and functional goals that will help the student be involved in and progress in the general education curriculum. The mandate for addressing transition services in students' IEPs has been changed from age 14 to no later than age 16. IDEA 2004 requires that a student's IEP be updated annually beginning at age 16 to address the following:

- Appropriate measurable postsecondary goals based upon age-appropriate transition assessments related to training, education, employment, and, where appropriate, independent living skills

- Transition services needed to assist the student to reach these goals including the student's course of study (e.g., career and technology education, college preparation courses)
- A statement that the student has been informed of the rights (if any) that will transfer to him or her on reaching the age of majority—no later than one year before reaching the age of majority under State law

Including students with disabilities in state and district assessments remains in IDEA 2004 and now requires that states develop accommodations guidelines. This is important in terms of assisting students to understand their needs and to request appropriate accommodations in secondary classes and for state and district assessments.

SUMMARY OF PERFORMANCE (SOP) REQUIREMENTS

IDEA 2004 includes a new mandate to provide each student with an SOP before he or she exits the school system (Section 614, Part B—Evaluations Before Change in Eligibility). As a student with a disability graduates from high school with a regular diploma or exceeds the age eligibility under state law, the local school system must provide a summary of

- The student's academic achievement and functional performance
- Recommendations on how to assist the student to meet his or her postsecondary goals

Transition assessment provides a way for students and practitioners to collect the information needed for this document. The SOP provides a way for school systems to compile assessment data and to provide students and their families with valuable information as they exit the school system. The SOP is explained in more detail in Chapter 7 and an example is included in Appendix A.

Assistive Technology

Assistive technology and the use of universal design is important in terms of accommodating students in general education, postsecondary education, and the community. The need for assistive technology for students with disabilities has been addressed in the IDEA Amendments of 1997, IDEA 2004, and the Assistive Technology Acts of 1998 and 2004. Specifically, assistive technology **devices** include commercial or customized equipment, items, or product systems that increase, maintain, or improve functional capabilities in students with disabilities. Assistive technology **services** include the selection, acquisition, or use of an assistive technology device, which can include a functional assessment of assistive technology in specific environments (e.g., workplace, general education, or postsecondary education classroom). Services also include information related to purchasing or leasing assistive technology devices, coordinating the use of assistive technology with education and rehabilitation plans, and training or technical assistance for students and family members.

Universal Design is a concept for designing and delivering products and services that are usable by all people. Products and services incorporating Universal Design can be used with or without assistive technologies. In education, Universal Design can be applied to learning by providing course instruction, materials, and content that promote equal access to learning for all students (e.g., textbook for history is made available in book format, in CD format with access to a computer, or on tape with access to headphones and tape player in the classroom). Therefore, students with disabilities or varying learning styles do not have to request accommodations but can choose the format that enhances their learning. Incorporating assistive technology and Universal Design into postsecondary education, employment, and community settings can assist students with disabilities to realize their postschool goals and participate as adults in their communities.

IDEA 2004 clearly provides a mandate for including transition assessment in the IEP process. The focus on students' needs, strengths, preferences, and interests provides an avenue for student choice in determining postschool goals. IDEA 2004 emphasizes the need for accommodations, assistive technology, and Universal Design to assist students in participating in state assessments, in general education, and in postsecondary environments. Legislation in the field of rehabilitation also addresses the need for accommodations in employment and community settings and provides an avenue for using transition assessment results. In the next section, this legislation is reviewed briefly as it relates to transition assessment.

OTHER SELECTED LEGISLATION IMPACTING TRANSITION ASSESSMENT

Legislation in the field of rehabilitation provides students with disabilities additional safeguards in school and adult life. Section 504 of the Rehabilitation Act of 1973 and the Americans with Disabilities Act (ADA) of 1990 provide students with the means to access programs, services, and accommodations if they are informed of and understand their rights under these laws.

Section 504

Section 504 of The Rehabilitation Act of 1973 (PL 93–112) is often regarded as landmark legislation impacting the civil rights of individuals with disabilities; programs and services receiving federal funds cannot discriminate against individuals on the basis of a disability. At the secondary level, some students with disabilities who are not eligible for special education services under IDEA 2004 may be eligible for reasonable accommodations under this law. These students may have a Section 504 Plan detailing accommodations needed in the general education classroom or to access the school building. While assessment data form the basis for determining eligibility for such reasonable accommodations, these students are not entitled to plan for transition services at age 16, as are students with an IEP.

It is important that all secondary students with disabilities (with an IEP or 504 Plan) understand that Section 504 provides the basis for requesting reasonable accommodations in postsecondary education and employment settings. In order to request accommodations, the student must self-disclose the presence of a disability and provide the rationale for asking for specific accommodations. This obviously requires students to understand their needs, strengths, preferences, and interests as discussed earlier in terms of transition assessment.

Americans with Disabilities Act

The Americans with Disabilities Act (ADA) also provides broad civil rights protection to individuals with disabilities in education, in employment, and in the community (e.g., transportation, recreational facilities, and telecommunications). The ADA extends Section 504 to the private sector in terms of access to and reasonable accommodations in these settings. Once again, individuals must understand their needs, strengths, preferences, and interests and match their characteristics with future education, employment, and community sites. For example, in terms of employment, it is important to note that only "qualified persons with disabilities" are entitled to protection from discrimination under ADA. This means individuals must be able to complete the essential functions of the job, which can be identified through a job analysis (see Appendix D). If the individual's needs, strengths, preferences, and interests match the requirements of the job, it is up to the student to disclose his or her disability and request reasonable accommodations under ADA if needed. If there is not a match between the individual and the essential functions of the job (e.g., student cannot lift 50 pounds for a warehouse position), then the individual would not be a "qualified person with a disability" under ADA.

Rehabilitation Amendments of 1998

The Rehabilitation Act Amendments of 1998 (Title IV of the Workforce Investment Act of 1998) are important in the transition assessment process in terms of using transition assessment results and finding out information on job-training opportunities in the community. First, it is possible to use transition assessment data collected during a student's secondary years to facilitate the eligibility and planning process in vocational rehabilitation. The Rehabilitation Amendments of 1998 specify that existing assessment data can be used for determining eligibility for services. School system personnel can compile transition assessment data and forward it to rehabilitation personnel with a student's permission (see Neubert & Moon, 2000, for an example) or share the SOP document (see Appendix A). Using existing assessment data during the eligibility process can be especially important for students with more significant disabilities; while these students may score poorly on traditional standardized tests, they may have demonstrated the ability to work in the community or attend supported postsecondary education classes. Once the individual is determined eligible for rehabilitation services, assessment data are also used to develop an individual plan for employment (IPE). The IPE outlines services and goals for the rehabilitation process and is similar to the IEP process in special education. Individual choice and self-determination are also emphasized in the rehabilitation process in that the IPE must be jointly developed between the counselor and the person with a disability.

Second, the Rehabilitation Act Amendments are part of the Workforce Investment Act of 1998 that now links a state's vocational rehabilitation system to a state's work force investment system (e.g., One Stop Career Centers). Students and/or practitioners should be able to access information about various job-training environments in the community to assist students in realizing postschool goals related to employment and advanced skill training. Appendix C provides a way to collect this information through a Community Assessment format.

SUMMARY

Transition assessment is an integral part of the educational process for students with disabilities during the secondary school years and serves as the foundation for planning for adult roles. Transition assessment encompasses age-appropriate methods to assist students in identifying individual needs, strengths, preferences, and interests and in obtaining information on future living, work, and education environments.

Deciding what to assess, who will assess, and how assessment data will be collected is critical during transition assessment. While there are a variety of methods associated with transition assessment, it is important for practitioners to determine what assessment data are needed at various transition points for each student and his or her family. Most important, data collected during the transition assessment process provide a foundation for secondary IEP development and for the SOP document. The chapters in this book provide a blueprint of how school personnel can approach these important tasks in transition assessment and enhance transition planning for students with disabilities. The essence of transition assessment is to make the best match for the student in terms of his or her individual characteristics and the demands of specific environments; this enhances access to and success in adult living, working, and learning environments.

REFERENCES

Americans with Disabilities Act of 1990, 42 U.S.C. § 12101 (1990).

Assistive Technology Act of 1998, 29 U.S.C. § 3001 (1998).

Assistive Technology Act of 2004, 29 U.S.C. § 3001 (2004).

Goals 2000: Educate America Act, 20 U.S.C. § 5801 (1994).

Halpern, A. S. (1994). The transition of youth with disabilities to adult life: A position of the Division on Career Development and Transition. *Career Development for Exceptional Individuals, 17,* 115–124.

Individuals with Disabilities Education Act, U.S.C. § 1401 (1990).

Individuals with Disabilities Education Act Amendments of 1997, 20 U.S.C. § 1400 (1997).

Individuals with Disabilities Education Improvement Act of 2004, 20 U.S.C. § 1400 (2004).

Neubert, D. A. (2003). The role of assessment in the transition to adult life process for individuals with disabilities. *Exceptionality, 11,* 63–71.

Neubert, D. A., & Moon, M. S. (2000). How a transition profile helps students prepare for life in the community. *Teaching Exceptional Children, 32*(2), 20–25.

No Child Left Behind Act, 20 U.S.C. § 6301 (2001).

Rehabilitation Act of 1973, 29 U.S.C. § 701 (1982).

School to Work Opportunities Act of 1994, 20 U.S.C. § 6101 (1994).

Sitlington, P. L., & Neubert, D. A. (1998). Assessment for life: Methods and processes to determine students' interests, abilities, and preferences. In M. Wehmeyer & D. J. Sands (Eds.), *Making it happen: Student involvement in educational planning, decision making, and instruction* (pp. 75–98). Baltimore: Brookes.

Sitlington, P. L., Neubert, D. A., Begun, W., Lombard, R. C., & Leconte, P. J. (1996). *Assess for success: Handbook on transition assessment.* Reston, VA: The Council for Exceptional Children.

Sitlington, P. L., Neubert, D. A., & Leconte, P. J. (1997). Transition assessment: The position of the Division on Career Development and Transition. *Career Development for Exceptional Individuals, 20,* 69–79.

Will, M. (1984). *OSERS programming for the transition of youth with disabilities: Bridges from school to working life.* Washington, DC: Office of Special Education and Rehabilitative Services.

Workforce Investment Act of 1998, 20 U.S.C. § 9201 (Title IV—Rehabilitation Amendments of 1998).

2

*Career Development
as a Context for
Transition Assessment*

This chapter provides an overview of the concept, phases, national standards and guidelines, and importance of career development as a context for appropriate transition assessment. The chapter goals are to

- Define career development
- Identify the phases of career development
- Identify national transition curricular standards and indicators concerning career development and transition assessment

Transition education and services necessarily broaden the scope of assessment. However, transition assessment continues to rest in part on a lifelong career development framework and within that context. Throughout students' education they move through a variety of transitions that help them prepare for and achieve major benchmarks and proceed to subsequent adult environments and challenges. As they leave school, they will assume new roles in postsecondary education, employment, maintaining a home, participating in the community, and enjoying personal and social relationships (Halpern, 1994). Each role is intrinsically linked to the others and plays a part in their overall career satisfaction and quality of life.

Assessment questions and activities address these diverse but interdependent roles to facilitate transition planning customized for each student. Regardless of the severity of students' disabilities, visions of themselves in these adult roles become crystallized by engaging in assessment activities—especially if they occur in a continuous fashion. Students identify more than career interests, abilities, aptitudes, temperaments, and values. Assessment affords them the opportunity to articulate dreams and goals. Planning to attain these requires assessment of their personal and social support networks, preferred leisure and recreational activities, understanding of health and wellness issues and needs, levels of community involvement, access to and abilities with transportation options, as well as family and living configurations, including the responsibilities of financial planning and management. Most of these assessment foci fall into five categories or standards for transition planning as developed via focus groups and analysis by national partners in the transition world (National Alliance for Secondary Education and Transition, 2005), which will be presented later in the chapter.

DEFINING CAREER DEVELOPMENT

Career development is "a continuous lifelong process of developmental experiences that focuses on seeking, obtaining and processing information about self, occupational educational alternatives, life styles, and role options" (Hansen, 1976 as cited in Morningstar, 1997, p. 315). Put another way, "career development is the process through which people come to understand themselves as they relate to the world of work and their role in it" (National Occupational Information Coordinating Committee, 1992, p. 3).

The career development process is facilitated by addressing all aspects of life within career contexts. Thus, family, social, and community influences may facilitate or interfere with natural progression within career development and expansion processes. Each person's process is personal and unique and involves making constant matching decisions. As part of "making the match" described in Chapter 7, levels of career development are assessed to identify the congruence or discrepancy between students' knowledge of themselves and their knowledge of various ecologies in which they now or may in the future operate. Knowledge of self includes but is not limited to the following attributes: values, preferences, nature of self-concept and level of self-esteem, abilities, attitudes, aptitudes, temperaments (e.g., personal disposition toward data, people, and things or various environments and work cultures), behaviors, needs, strengths, interests, and skills.

Students need guidance and support traversing through the career development process. The "can-do's" identified in Figure 2.1: Career Development Checklist, may provide a starting point for determining what phase students are in and the types of assessment that could facilitate movement from one level to another. The checklist is not exhaustive and

Figure 2.1   Career Development Checklist

Career Awareness
- Can identify parents' and other family members' jobs.
- Can describe what parents and others do on their jobs.
- Can name and describe at least 10 different occupations.
- Can describe how people get jobs.
- Can describe at least three jobs to investigate.
- Can discuss what happens if adults cannot or do not work.
- Can identify why people have to get along with each other at work.

Career Exploration
- Can discern the difference between a job and a career.
- Can identify three ways to find out about different occupations.
- Can state at least three things they want in a job.
- Can identify the steps in finding a job.
- Can identify at least three careers they want to explore.
- Can state preferences for indoor vs. outdoor work, solitary work vs. working with others, and working with their hands and tools/machines versus working strictly with their minds.
- Can identify how to get applications and how to complete them.
- Can discuss why interviews are important.
- Can identify their strengths, abilities, skills, learning styles, and special needs regarding work or specific jobs.

Career Preparation
- Can identify career/vocational courses they want to take in school.
- Can describe the educational and work requirements of specific careers and jobs.
- Can identify where education and training can be obtained.
- Can explain steps in acquiring the skills necessary to enter a chosen field or job.
- Can describe entry-level skills, course or job requirements, and exit-level competencies to succeed in courses.
- Can identify community and educational options and alternatives to gaining education and employment in a chosen field.
- Can identify the worker characteristics and skills in working with others that are required in a chosen field or job.

Career Assimilation
- Can identify steps to take if they want to advance in their place of employment.
- Can identify educational benefits and ways of gaining additional training through their employment.
- Can explain fields related to their current work into which they could transfer.
- Can identify ways to change jobs without losing benefits or salary.
- Can describe appropriate ways of leaving or changing jobs and companies.
- Can relate their skills to other occupations and avocations.
- Can explain retirement benefits.
- Can identify and participate in leisure activities that they can pursue after they retire.

will vary within different cultural contexts, but the examples could serve as benchmarks to be checked—and rechecked, periodically—to recognize where students are in the recursive and cyclical process. Students can use the checklist to verify their progression through the four career-development phases.

CAREER DEVELOPMENT PHASES

Career development is a personal, iterative, and reiterative process. Though it is often presented as a linear sequence, it is cumulative, but learning continues as one discovers new areas to explore or as one is required to adapt to changes in the world of work. The process includes

- Career awareness
- Career exploration
- Career preparation
- Career assimilation

Brolin identified the fourth phase, assimilation, as comprising "placement, follow-up, and continuing education" (1993, p. 2). Lately this has been expanded to include the ability to adapt to changes in one's adult work roles: changing positions within a career, moving up the career ladder, transferring from one role in a career to another, changing careers entirely, or eventually retiring (Leconte, 1994). These changes or transitions require ongoing learning. Assessment for transition is needed during the lifelong career development process whenever any change is expected (e.g., moving from middle school to high school, graduating from high school to attend college), imminent (e.g., changing from service learning to work experience, being laid off), or planned (e.g., projecting course sequences that integrate career technical education with academic requirements, designing a major in college). All these changes involve moving from one environment, situation, or status to another. Career awareness begins the lifelong journey.

Career Awareness

The initial phase begins as students discover the existence of work, jobs, various careers as well as college and other postsecondary education options, and participating in community and leisure activities. Usually this phase occurs as students move from protected worlds at home, day care, and preschool to the new settings of schooling and community. Again, awareness based on new discoveries happens throughout life. Career-education activities such as educational visits to fire stations, companies, and offices promote awareness (Amos, 2006). These trips and visits by professionals to classrooms are designed to expand self-awareness ("would I like to work there?" or "I want to be like the park ranger who came to tell us what she does" or "it would be fun to drive a truck") and knowledge of community occupations, how they fit into the fabric of society, and how people have to get along with others (Brolin & Loyd, 2004; Levinson, 1993).

The awareness phase includes making cause-and-effect connections (e.g., people work to earn money to acquire material goods; people who live on their own must pay to live that way). Later, more complex connections are made, such as working to accomplish things one believes in or doing something that one enjoys (Herr, Kramer, & Niles, 2004).

Career Awareness

Marcus is a nineteen-year-old student with severe cognitive disabilities who spends his time playing with his elementary-school-aged neighbors; he is not required to do any household chores. His teachers and parents are encouraging him to make career decisions and specific job choices for the summer. All are becoming frustrated because he does not perform on job trials in the community and because he voices his dislike for all the jobs he has tried. In his case, people did not "start where he is" within the career development phases; rather, they jumped into activities that could be appropriate for his chronological age but not for his level of cognitive functioning or for his level of understanding about work, jobs, and careers. First, his parents, teachers, and counselor should introduce him to the nature of work, what jobs are and what they require, and the demands and responsibilities of performing chores. His curriculum and assessment should focus on (a) his understanding of what work requires of him, (b) the knowledge that eventually he will be seeking work, (c) how he views himself working, and (d) where he envisions working.

Sample questions that educators and parents can ask students to determine career awareness are contained in Figure 2.2: Relevant Assessment Questions for Career Development. If students have not gained sufficient awareness of the world of careers and work, they may have difficulty moving into the next phase, career exploration.

Career Exploration

The second phase of career development involves students interacting physically, emotionally, and behaviorally as much as possible with various aspects of work in different occupational or career areas. Students also learn about postsecondary options and the differences in lifestyles of workers who possess high-level skills compared with those who have lesser skills. Educational and family activities such as accompanying adults to work,

Figure 2.2   Relevant Assessment Questions for Career Development

Awareness Phase
- What is work?
- What is a job?
- What are some jobs you know about?
- What kind of work do people do on these jobs?
- What have you dreamed of doing when you finish school?
- What kind of job do you want?
- Where do you want to live, and with whom, when you are grown up?
- Why do people work? Why do you want to work?
- What do you enjoy doing when you are not in school?
- What jobs do your mother, father, and other family members have?
- What types of things do they do on their jobs?
- What is college? Why do people go to college? What is vocational training?
- What is public transportation? How would you get where you want to go if your parents did not drive you?
- What is voting?

Exploration Phase
- What jobs are you interested in visiting?
- What exploratory courses would you like to take in school?
- What hobbies do you have?
- What activities do you do in your spare time?
- What volunteer or community service work do you do?
- Did you enjoy your summer job? What parts did you like best?
- Do you like being inside or outside better?
- Do you prefer being with other people, or do you enjoy being by yourself?
- Do you enjoy working with your hands and with tools, or do you prefer to solve problems in your head?
- Did you get along well with your classmates? If so, why did you? If not, why didn't you?
- What skills do you have that you can use in these or other courses?

Preparation Phase
- What courses do you need to achieve your career goals?
- What skills will you need to gain entry into those courses?
- How will you prepare to live on your own?
- Will you need to take courses during high school and after?
- Will these courses lead to college courses? Does the school have a tech prep program?
- Do you and your family plan for you to attend college?
- Will you gain the skills needed to succeed in college?
- Will you be able to get a job based on your high school and/or college coursework?
- Does the educational program provide job placement and support?
- Can you gain entry into an approved apprenticeship program?

Assimilation Phase
- Can you continue your training and education after you begin employment?
- Does the employer provide educational benefits?
- How can you advance within the company?
- Can you transfer between departments in your company?
- Does the employer offer a good retirement and benefits package?
- Do you have alternatives to pursue if your employer has to downsize or lay off workers?
- Do you have options for continuing education, even for leisure interests?
- Can you transfer your job skills and avocational skills to other employment?

trying different courses in school, shadowing workers, and actually working via service learning, work experience, or part-time jobs are ways to facilitate exploration and assessment (Dykeman, et al., 2003). Visits to career technical centers and programs as well as participation in community-based assessments (e.g., situational assessments, on-the-job tryouts) are appropriate during this phase. Such activities provide students with the knowledge and skills to refine their attitudes toward work and encourage them to develop decision-making skills, connect educational requirements to those of different occupations or careers, and begin to create personal career plans (Brolin & Loyd, 2004; Levinson, 1993). Students begin identifying their interests and abilities in relation to school courses that will help them prepare for certain careers.

Career Exploration

Estella, a seventeen-year-old junior with mild cerebral palsy, is ready to explore more courses and eventual careers because she has enjoyed her school electives (e.g., art, keyboarding, and computer applications). She has visited with various family members and friends on their jobs, volunteered at a computer camp for elementary students, and job-shadowed workers at a large graphic arts company. Her jobs the past two summers at a coffee bar and as an assistant camp counselor helped her decide that she preferred working with computers more than serving or working with people. Additionally, she accessed the state career information system in the career center at school and discussed the advantages and disadvantages of attending the community college or the local university. Although her performances in all classes are satisfactory and she took the SAT, she is uncertain about her direction. She opts to participate in additional assessment to learn more about her preferences and abilities. During the assessment process, she discovers that she can combine her talent in art with her abilities and interest in computers. Also, she learned about assistive technology that helps her operate computers more quickly and easily. Finally, she decides to take a computer-assisted graphic arts course during senior year and then attend the community college to gain a graphic arts certificate and her associate's degree. Having met the Disability Student Services coordinator on a tour of the community college with her parents, she feels comfortable discussing accommodations she will need. After she graduates and works a while, she may attend the university.

Questions suitable to ask students in the career exploration phase are included in Figure 2.2: Relevant Assessment Questions for Career Development. If students respond to these questions satisfactorily, they can move into the career preparation phase.

Career Preparation

The third phase of career development, career preparation, involves acquiring career and vocationally related knowledge and skills. The goals for this phase include identifying and developing transferable and vocationally specific skills, and continuing to develop employability or soft skills, such as problem-solving, adapting to change, working cooperatively with others, and as a member of a team (SCANS, 1991). Students begin to experience activities that earn wages, participate in work and community cultures, manage paychecks and finances, and provide or access their own transportation. They also refine their career goals in terms of enrolling in career-oriented courses in secondary and postsecondary education and plot out paths to attain long-term goals.

Career and technical education (CTE) or vocational education serves as a major factor in this phase as courses and programs of study are designed to prepare students to become productive, skilled citizens. By participating in career clusters and/or academies at the secondary level, students gain academic, vocational, and SCANS skills that can lead to employment and postsecondary education. Through their engagement in CTE, students begin to clarify their preferences and compatibilities with other adult roles (e.g., taxpayer, coworker, employee, voter).

Career Preparation

After taking interest inventories in middle school and another interest inventory and an aptitude test in ninth grade, LeRoy did not know "what he wanted to do" regarding a career, partly because no one shared the results of the assessments with him or his grandmother. His learning disability impeded his learning until last year when his new teachers referred him for a diagnostic evaluation. Now he uses a text-to-speech reader, has his textbooks available to download onto his iPod, receives accommodations on tests, and is more motivated to earn good grades so that he "can own a business in about ten years." His counselor helped him explore different careers using the O*NET and America's Career Resource Network on the Web. One Saturday he took the ASVAB (Armed Services Vocational Aptitude Battery) and discovered he has potential to learn drafting and several other occupational areas. LeRoy worked as a custodian with his grandmother's employer and for a florist. After a florist's assistant was sick the day before a holiday, he helped create arrangements and has been doing so for over a year after school. Last summer he worked with a local landscaper, because he enjoys working outdoors; he works there on Saturdays and plans to return next summer. The landscaper said she would hire him when he graduates if he would enroll in the Horticulture and Landscaping career technical program in the school district. He enjoys the program, is earning good grades, and plans to squeeze in a marketing course during his senior year to help prepare him for owning a business. The landscaper told him that when he is ready, he can attend special programs or courses offered by the Small Business Administration to learn more about setting up and operating a successful business.

CTE provides a variety of organized educational activities that

- offer a sequence of courses that provides individuals with the academic and technical knowledge and skills for careers (other than careers requiring a baccalaureate, master's, or doctoral degree) in current or emerging employment sectors; and
- include competency-based applied learning that contributes to the academic knowledge, higher-order reasoning and problem-solving skills, work attitudes, general employability skills, technical skills, and occupation-specific skills of an individual (Carl D. Perkins Vocational and Technical Education Act of 1998).

CTE programs are most often categorized within career clusters such as the following:

- Arts and Communications
- Business, Management, and Computer Technology
- Health Services
- Human Services
- Engineering and Industrial Technology
- Natural Resources and Environmental Sciences (America's Career Resource Network, n.d.)

Courses such as graphic arts, drafting, marketing, practical nursing, law enforcement, child care services, auto technology, carpentry, and welding are divided into these six clusters.

Students may opt not to participate in CTE or may take one or two unrelated CTE courses during high school (e.g., Web design, Introduction to Business, computer-aided drafting). Because CTE students engage in school (classroom-based) and community (work-based) activities, research shows that they may have greater employment stability and higher earning power following their education. A second advantage of CTE participation involves developmental, long-term preparation for careers and employment versus short-term, job skill training that drives job training programs that might be provided by unions, large companies, work force development programs, trade associations, or rehabilitation agencies. The latter usually provide basic and entry-level skills that then require people to gain additional skills through on-the-job training. People can also learn skills entirely on the job. Table 2.1: Relationship of Career Preparation Pathways to Outcomes depicts both short-term and long-term results for students.

Table 2.1   Relationship of Career Preparation Pathways to Outcomes

Preparation Options	*Career-related Outcomes*
Career Technical Education ----------- *Programs* 2 to 3 years in high school and / or postsecondary education	Long-term career development plus vocationally specific skill sets
Career Technical Education ----------- *courses* in high school, community college, or adult education	Specific skill sets (e.g., Web design) (can enhance employment or postsecondary education)
Work force development ----------- courses or training	Basic or entry-level skills that can be used on occupationally specific jobs (Microsoft Office, roofing, home health care aide)
On-the-job training -----------	Entry-level skills for specific jobs

Questions suitable to ask students in the career preparation phase are included in Figure 2.2: Relevant Assessment Questions for Career Development. If students respond to these questions satisfactorily, they will have a better chance of succeeding in their career pursuits as well as in career assimilation.

Career Assimilation

Career assimilation is the fourth phase of career development and requires many SCANS skills and competencies (1991), particularly the ability for lifelong learning and adaptability. No longer can employees rely on job stability. The nature of jobs (and work) changes so rapidly that students must be prepared to shift from old methods of working to new, from not using much technology to relying on it, from knowing one job to knowing several, and from simply following others' orders to directing their own career trajectories and designing new ways to be productive.

Career assimilation means one can blend into the workforce as a team player who can self-initiate and who can move easily between positions or workplaces, both laterally and vertically. The transition process for today's and tomorrow's employees means losing jobs, changing jobs or positions, and seeking advancement. Tomorrow's jobs will disappear as rapidly as new types of work develop (Bridges, 1994; Karoly & Panis, 2004); today's students should be preparing for new workplaces. Assessment for these transitions is as critical as those associated with previous career development phases. Students with disabilities may need to revisit assessment periodically, partly because some students may face challenges adapting to change, generalizing job-seeking skills, or learning new work cultures and environments. Students can begin to prepare for this phase and all that it entails while still in school. In fact, assessment should be designed around some of these issues to help students identify what works for them and what they still need to learn.

Career Assimilation

Amanda, who is twenty and has an acquired brain injury, participates in a postsecondary program operated collaboratively between the school system (where she attended school until last year) and the local community college. She worked in an animal shelter for three months, but the owner had to lay her off because she missed too much time (due to being late and missing the bus). She had to revisit the decision-making process for seeking new employment that she would enjoy. This required her to review abilities and interests to perform in different work environments, to re-engage in job-seeking skills, and to look for jobs that she could access by public transportation.

Together Amanda, her transition coordinator, and rehabilitation counselor decided that she should participate in a number of community-based work experiences or job try-outs. After being assessed and trying out work as a teacher's aide, an assistant to a dog groomer, a courier in a local company, an aide in one of the community college offices, and as sorter in a clothing store, she decided that she enjoyed and could perform tasks at a school for guide dogs. The job site is one block from a bus stop and she now lives with a friend who helps her wake up in time for work. Eventually, support from her transition coordinator will fade as will her rehabilitation services. She will then rely on her skills and her self-identified network of friends, family, and social supports.

Questions suitable to ask students in the career assimilation phase are included in Figure 2.2: Relevant Assessment Questions for Career Development. If students respond to these questions knowledgably, they may successfully navigate the challenges presented by job changes or loss.

CAREER PATHWAYS AND DECISION MAKING

All students can access and take part in the career pathways of moving through the phases of career awareness (self-knowledge and career knowledge), career exploration (building academic foundations, investigating, and participating in exploratory activities such as job shadowing), and career preparation, including career cluster selection, advanced academic skill development, and related work experience (Maryland State Department of Education, 1998). Often these phases are depicted as occurring in elementary school (awareness), middle or junior high school (exploration), and high school (preparation), but this linear, sequential portrayal can be misleading. As students move through their school years, the career development process can be repeated indefinitely, although with each iteration, they accumulate knowledge and skills. Following kindergarten through high school years, they have options available that include immediate job entry, community college, career technical proprietary school, work force development training programs, four-year colleges and advanced academic degree preparation. From these preparatory settings, students move into entry-level employment or technical or professional careers, and hopefully they are prepared to learn continuously, to adapt to change, to be flexible in their working approaches and decision making. With these skills, they should enjoy productive, meaningful, and satisfying work and lives.

STANDARDS FOR TRANSITION ASSESSMENT

Various assessment areas and contexts, designed to both gauge and foster career development levels, align with the *National Standards and Quality Indicators for Secondary Education and Transition* (National Alliance for Secondary Education and Transition, 2005)—for all students. The standards, which are mirrored in the *Guideposts for Success* developed by the National Collaborative on Workforce and Disability (National Collaborative on Workforce and Disability for Youth, 2005), address the broad categories of

- Schooling or school preparation
- Career preparatory experiences
- Youth development and leadership
- Family involvement, and
- Connecting activities

The term "connecting activities" refers to "a flexible set of services, accommodations, and supports that help youth gain access to and achieve success within chosen postschool options" (National Alliance on Secondary Education and Transition, 2005, p. 12).

NEED FOR ASSESSMENT
OF CAREER DEVELOPMENT

Each standard is of equal importance, but assessment for career development and preparation is often the most challenging to provide in a meaningful way (Dykeman et al., 2003; Hughes & Karp, 2004). In fact, research shows that students in the United States "simply are not getting enough of . . . [career development] intervention[s]" (Dykeman et al., 2003, p. 1). Students with disabilities receive even fewer career development interventions from traditional sources such as school counselors than do their peers without disabilities (Johnson, et al., 2006; HEATH Resource Center, 2006). Increasingly, students are responsible for conducting career assessments themselves via Web-based or computer-based career assessment programs (Hughes & Karp, 2004). This trend may not be as helpful for students with disabilities as for their nondisabled peers. Assessment is one of many career development interventions (Dykeman, et al., 2001; Leconte, 1994) but it is often viewed as complicated or difficult to provide. Hopefully, readers of this publication will view assessment as critical and easy to provide, especially within the career development context. Aligning assessment with current standards may help educators integrate career development and transition standards with federal and state testing requirements.

STANDARDS PERTAINING TO
CAREER DEVELOPMENT

The standards "identify what is needed for youth to participate successfully in postsecondary education and training, civic engagement, meaningful employment, and adult life" (National Alliance for Secondary Education and Transition, 2005, p. 1). This chapter focuses on assessment for career development (regarding the second standard) which is described in Figure 2.3: Standards and Indicators for Career Preparatory Experiences.

Though the Standards and Indicators mention assessment as part of curriculum goals for students (e.g., Indicator 2.2.2, Indicator 2.4.2.), developing questions for each indicator is also important for designing assessment within the entire career category. Questions to pose for each indicator include

- Do we provide this?
- If we do not provide this, how can we do so in an expedited manner?
- Do we offer sufficient variety (to include all possibilities)?
- Do we offer these often and with enough variety to reach every student?
- Do we truly include both youth and their families in these experiences?
- Do we provide opportunities within school and community contexts?

Figure 2.3   Standards and Indicators for Career Preparatory Experiences

2.1.	**Youth participate in career awareness, exploration, and preparatory activities in school- and community-based settings.**
2.1.1.	Schools and community partners offer courses, programs, and activities that broaden and deepen youths' knowledge of careers and allow for more informed postsecondary educational and career choices.
2.1.2.	Career preparatory courses (as in courses of study required by IDEA 2004), programs, and activities incorporate contextual teaching and learning.
2.1.3.	Schools, employers, and community partners collaboratively plan and design career preparatory courses, programs, and activities that support quality standards, practices, and experiences.
2.1.4.	Youth and families understand the relationship between postsecondary education and career choices, and the role of financial and benefits planning.
2.1.5.	Youth understand how community resources, nonwork experiences, and family members can assist them in their role as workers.
2.2.	**Academic and nonacademic courses and programs include integrated career development activities.**
2.2.1.	Schools offer broad career curricula that allow youth to organize and select academic, career, and/or technical courses based on their career interests and goals.
2.2.2.	With the guidance of school and/or community professionals, youth use a career planning process (e.g., assessments, career portfolios) incorporating their career goals, interests, and abilities.
2.2.3.	Career preparatory courses, programs, and activities align with labor market trends and up-to-date job requirements.
2.2.4.	Career preparatory courses, programs, and activities provide the basic skills needed for success in a career field and the prerequisites for further training and professional growth.
2.3.	**Schools and community partners provide youth with opportunities to participate in meaningful school- and community-based work experiences.**
2.3.1.	Youth participate in high-quality work experiences that are offered to them prior to completing high school (e.g., apprenticeships, mentoring, paid and unpaid work, service learning, school-based enterprises, on-the-job training, internships).
2.3.2.	Work experiences are relevant and aligned with each youth's career interests, postsecondary education plans, goals, skills, abilities, and strengths.
2.3.3.	Youth participate in various on-the-job training experiences, including community service (paid or unpaid) specifically linked to school credit or program content.
2.3.4.	Youth are able to access, accept, and use individually needed supports and accommodations for work experiences.
2.4.	**Schools and community partners provide career preparatory activities that lead to youths' acquisition of employability and technical skills, knowledge, and behaviors.**
2.4.1.	Youth have multiple opportunities to develop traditional job preparation skills through job-readiness curricula and training.
2.4.2.	Youth complete career assessments to identify school and postschool preferences, interests, skills, and abilities.
2.4.3.	Youth exhibit understanding of career expectations, workplace culture, and the changing nature of work and educational requirements.
2.4.4.	Youth demonstrate that they understand how personal skills and characteristics (e.g., positive attitude, self-discipline, honesty, time management) affect their employability.
2.4.5.	Youth demonstrate appropriate job-seeking behaviors.

SOURCE: National Alliance on Secondary Education and Transition, 2005, p. 6–7.

The Standards document includes a self-assessment tool for transition-team partners that recommends a rating format for each indicator ranging from *always evident*, to *never evident*. These are designed for the entire system, which is critical, but in this publication we want to ensure that options are in place so that questions can be asked for each individual student in the system. To make sure that all students make progress through each career development phase, initial questions should be asked (e.g., "do you like to be and work with others, or would you prefer to work alone?" or "do you know why people work?"). These will establish baseline information about the extent and depth of their self-knowledge as it pertains to their evolving career knowledge and preparation. Baseline information should be included in their Individual Education Program plans at least annually.

ALIGNING NATIONAL TRANSITION STANDARDS WITH PHASES OF CAREER DEVELOPMENT

Suggested student questions include those in Figure 2.1: Career Development Checklist, which encompass the career preparatory experiences described in the above-mentioned standards and indicators and which follow the traditional phases of career development: awareness, exploration, preparation, and assimilation. Student responses to these questions should be tracked to determine their progress in refining their career understanding and planning next steps in transition assessment. The questions included in Figure 2.1 follow the path of career development that all persons must travel to gain career satisfaction. Because students will constantly discover new career information, their paths will be reiterative—meaning they may cycle through exploration and preparation at various stages of their development during their lives.

ALIGNING NATIONAL CAREER DEVELOPMENT GUIDELINES WITH CAREER DEVELOPMENT

The National Career Development Guidelines (NCDG) that the National Career Development Association along with government entities (e.g., America's Career Resources Network sponsored by the U.S. Department of Education's Office of Vocational and Adult Education) encourage schools to follow, provide yet a different, but related, framework from which students and their transition teams can develop goals and objectives for IEPs. By using the NCDG standards and indicators they can verify that they are attending to multiple activities that promote career development. The Guidelines are available on the America's Career Resources Network Web site provided in the Additional Resources section of this chapter.

Built upon the previous competencies developed by the National Occupational Information Coordinating Committee, the term "competency" has been changed to "standard." The purpose of the standards and indicators is to

create high quality career development programs for youth and adults in a variety of settings that

- Help students acquire skills they will need to transition successfully to postsecondary training or a job after high school
- Help students achieve more by linking classroom study to future choices, and
- Help adults acquire new skills and move through career transitions (America's Career Resource Network, n.d.)

The NCDG encompass individuals and their ecologies, but they treat them within a different framework of standards and indicators. When examined closely the NCDG provide detailed guidance for exactly what students should be able to do regarding the three standards of Personal Social Development (previously known as "self-knowledge" in the 1989 NCDG standards), Education and Lifelong Learning (previously identified as "educational and occupational exploration" in the 1989 standards), and Career Management (previously called "career planning" in the old standards).

Regardless of the standards used, it is apparent that educators and others believe career development is an integral part of education and that it fosters long-term employment and quality of life.

SUMMARY

Students traverse through their personal career development process to form a unique career identity. Not everyone moves at the same rate or has the same needs or goals. It is imperative that students and their transition teams identify "where they are" in the career development process of awareness, exploration, preparation, and assimilation. Are they in the awareness phase although they are in high school? Are they in the preparation phase while in a transition program between high school and postsecondary options? Can they, according to the National Career Development Guidelines, demonstrate their ability to seek assistance from appropriate resources including other people (an "application" indicator within the Personal Social Development Standard)? Can they "evaluate the impact of past decisions on their current chances" (a "reflection" indicator within the Career Management Standard)?

We typically think of the first three phases being experienced prior to and during school, but as stated earlier, careers and occupations change so rapidly now that people are engaged continually in awareness, exploration, and preparation long after they leave school. Being employed does not provide the stability it once did; in current times, retaining employment means knowing how to learn and continuously doing so. In fact, this is one factor included in the SCANS report (1991) to which all potential workers should subscribe. Assessment for transition includes assessing change and transition junctures within each career development process as well as throughout working lives. Effective assessment is individualized and ongoing to provide a maximum of information required for students to make the match between their interests, needs, preferences, and goals and options that exist in their many ecologies of school, community, employment and, eventually, adult life. To ensure that career development is not a single event or one-time activity, students must learn early that they have multiple pathways to make their own decisions, to sustain personal growth, and to be empowered—or call the shots for their lives.

REFERENCES

America's Career Resource Network. (n.d.). *The national career development guidelines.* Retrieved March 2, 2006, from http://www.acrnetwork.org/ncdg.htm

Amos, B. (2006). Grades K-8 in the transition process: A critical foundation. In P. L. Sitlington & G. M. Clark (Eds.), *Transition education and services for students with disabilities* (pp. 109–126). Boston: Pearson/Allyn & Bacon.

Bridges, W. (1994). *JobShift: How to prosper in a workplace without jobs.* Reading, MA: Addison-Wesley.

Brolin, D. E. (1993). *Life centered career education: A competency based approach* (4th ed.). Arlington, VA: The Council for Exceptional Children.

Brolin, D. E., & Loyd, R. J. (2004). *Career development and transition services: functional life skills approach.* Upper Saddle River, NJ: Pearson/Merrill, Prentice, Hall.

Carl D. Perkins Vocational and Technical Education Act of 1998, 20 USC 2302 *et seq.*

Clark, D. (1999). *Bloom's taxonomy.* Retrieved March 2, 2006, from http://www.officeport.com/edu/blooms.htm

Clark, G. M., & Kolsote, O. P. (1995). *Career development and transition education for adolescents with disabilities.* Boston: Allyn & Bacon.

Dykeman, C., Herr, E. L., Ingram, M., Pehrsson, D., Wood, C., & Charles, S. (2001). *A taxonomy of career development interventions that occur in U.S. secondary schools.* Minneapolis, MN: National Research Center for Career and Technical Education, University of Minnesota.

Dykeman, C., Wood, C., Ingram, M., Gitelman, A., Mandsager, N., Chen, M., & Herr, E. L. (2003). *Career development interventions and academic self-efficacy and motivation: A pilot study.* St. Paul, MN: National Research Center for Career and Technical Education, University of Minnesota.

Halpern, A. S. (1994). The transition of youth with disabilities to adult life: A position statement of the Division of Career Development and Transition. *Career Development for Exceptional Individuals, 17,* 115–124.

HEATH Resource Center: National Clearinghouse on Postsecondary Education for Individuals with Disabilities. (2006, March). *Guidance and career counselors' toolkit: Advising high school students with disabilities on postsecondary options.* Washington, DC: Author, The George Washington University.

Herr, E. L., Cramer, S. H., & Niles, S. G. (2004). *Career guidance and counseling through the lifespan: Systematic Approaches* (6th ed.). Boston: Pearson/Allyn & Bacon.

Hughes, K. L., & Karp, M. M. (2004). *School-based career development: A synthesis of the literature.* New York, NY: Institute on Education and the Economy, Teachers College, Columbia University.

Johnson, L., Cabriele, M., Smith, L., Woldehanna, R., Leconte, P., & Rothenbacher, C. (2006, March). Career assessment and exploration for youth. Presentation at the Virginia Transition Forum in Roanoke, Virginia.

Karoly, L. A., & Panis, C. (2004). *The 21st century at work: Forces shaping the future workforce and workplace in the United States.* Retrieved April 19, 2006 from http://www.rand.org/pubs/monographs/MG164/index.html

Leconte, P. J. (1994). *A perspective on vocational appraisal: Beliefs, practices, and paradigms.* Unpublished doctoral dissertation, The George Washington University, Washington, DC.

Levinson, E. M. (1993). *Transdisciplinary vocational assessment: Issues in school-based programs.* Brandon, VT: Clinical Psychology Publishing.

Maryland State Department of Education. (1998). *Career pathways.* Unpublished document. Baltimore: Author.

Morningstar, M. E. (1997). Critical issues in career development and employment preparation for adolescents with disabilities. *Remedial and Special Education, 18*(5), 307–320.

National Alliance for Secondary Education and Transition. (2005). *National standards and quality indicators: Transition toolkit for systems improvement.* Minneapolis, MN: University of Minnesota, National Center on Secondary Education and Transition.

National Collaborative on Workforce and Disability for Youth. (2005). *Guideposts for success.* Washington, DC: Author.

National Occupational Information Coordinating Committee. (1992). *The national career development guidelines.* Washington, DC: Author.

Secretaries Commission on Achieving Necessary Skills. (1991). *What work requires of schools: A SCANS report for America 2000.* Washington, DC: U.S. Department of Labor.

ADDITIONAL RESOURCES

A Parent Handbook for Career Development. Available from http://www.acrnet work.org/resourcedetail.aspx?ID=200104

America's Career Resources Network. http://www.acrnetwork.org

Timmons, J., Podmostko, M., Bremer, C., Lavin, D., & Wills, J. (2004). *Career planning begins with assessment: A guide for professionals serving youth with educational and career development challenges.* Washington, DC: National Collaborative on Workforce and Disability for Youth and Institute for Educational Leadership.

3

The Role of Self-Determination in the Transition Assessment Process

Student-centered planning is a central theme of transition assessment activities. Although there is widespread support for assessing and teaching self-determination skills to students with disabilities in American schools, there is little evidence that instruction in these skills has been fully integrated into public school curricula (Test et al., 2004). Students with disabilities can and must be taught to be active participants in the transition assessment and planning process. The Individuals With Disabilities Education Improvement Act of 2004 (IDEA 2004) requires that students 16 and older be invited to participate in meetings where their individualized education programs (IEPs) are being developed and that transition planning be based in part on the students' interests and needs. Despite this legislation, students with disabilities have not been active participants in IEP and other related educational planning activities. A study by Wehmeyer and Schwartz (1998), for example, found that 31% of teachers reported that they did not include any self-determination goals on student IEPs and another 41% of teachers reported they lacked adequate knowledge or train-ing to teach self-determination to students with disabilities. Moreover, studies conducted between 1994 and 2004 reveal that only 48% to 64% of adolescents with disabilities attend their IEP meetings (Test et al., 2004). Students with mild, moderate, or severe disabilities must all be provided the opportunity for making choices and goal setting. Students and family members must be included as integral members of the assessment and planning team if meaningful adult outcomes are to be realized after high school departure. Accordingly, the purpose of this chapter is to:

- Explore self-determination in relation to transition assessment and goal setting
- Provide examples of student involvement on the assessment team
- Explore strategies for assessing and developing self-determination skills
- Demonstrate the relationship between self-determination, transition assessment, and goal setting

Issues pertaining to self-determination have been a central focus since the Individuals With Disabilities Education Act of 1990 (IDEA). This act stated that students must be invited to the IEP and transition planning meeting and that the coordinated set of activities that comprise the transi-tion component of the IEP "must be based on the individual student's needs, taking into account the student's preferences and interests" [300.18(b)(1)]. Since then the IDEA Amendments of 1997 and IDEA 2004 have reinforced these concepts. In particular, IDEA 2004 mandates that transition services be "based on the individual child's needs, taking into account the child's strengths, preferences and interests" [602(34)(B)].

Due to this emphasis, each student with disabilities must be prepared to become a fully empowered member of the IEP team and to provide input based on information gained through transition assessment proce-dures. Martin et al. (1997) developed an eleven-step program to prepare students with disabilities to participate fully in the goal-setting process during the development of their IEP. This program, known as the Self-Directed IEP, assumes that students must be taught eleven specific skills before they can become active participants in the IEP goal-setting process. Miller, Lombard, and Corbey (2007) suggested that educational goal-setting and student involvement in problem solving and decision making during the IEP process is a critical component of self-determination. In addition, Miller et al. proposed a transition assessment model that includes five assessment areas. They include the following: assessment of future plans, assessment of self-determination and self-advocacy, assess-ment of academic and behavioral skills, assessment of life skills, and assessment of vocational skills including interests, abilities, and aptitudes.

In this assessment model, self-determination and self-advocacy represent key and essential components of the comprehensive transition assessment process.

Educational assessment has always been an integral component of the U.S. school system. Unfortunately, the students who are the "subject" of assessment often become the "object" of assessment (Halpern, 1994). Students with disabilities are often the passive recipients of assessment activities and seldom see any relevance to their daily lives. They are seldom made aware of the purposes of assessment or take an active role in posing the questions to be answered as a result of assessment procedures. Traditional assessment and testing typically use a vernacular that is familiar to educators, but is not understood by students or their families. This is due, in part, to the fact that educators historically have assumed sole responsibility for test administration, test interpretation, and all curriculum and placement decisions that were made as a result of testing. Students with disabilities and their families were not considered to be important participants in this process. The opportunity now exists through transition assessment to "alter the 'locus of interpretation' from the examiner to the person being assessed" (Halpern, 1994, p. 119). Students must be prepared to conduct self-evaluations, interpret assessment results, and create educational goals that are based on assessment information. To achieve these goals, transition assessment approaches must address the preparation of students to become active players on assessment and planning teams.

Data generated through transition assessment activities must be made available to the student and presented in a context that is readily interpreted by the student. For example, information compiled as a result of standardized testing may mean very little to a student unless the results are discussed within the context of that student's personal aspirations and educational goals. Student-centered transition planning must be based upon an individual's awareness of his or her present level of functioning, a personal vision for the future, and knowing what must be done to get where he or she wants to be. Mithaug (1993) asks this question of students: "What are you willing and able to do to get what you haven't got?"

Wehmeyer (1996) defined self-determination as "acting as the primary causal agent in one's life and making choices and decisions regarding one's quality of life free from undue external influence or interference" (p. 22). Wehmeyer postulates that the self-determined individual exhibits four behavioral characteristics: (1) acts autonomously, (2) is self-regulated, (3) initiates and responds to events in a psychologically empowered manner, and (4) acts in a self-realized manner. Self-actualization is defined as realizing one's potential and living life accordingly. Any assessment activities that focus on self-determination and self-advocacy skills should include the four characteristics identified above.

Yet another definition of self-determination is supported by the Division on Career Development and Transition (DCDT).

> Self-determination is a combination of skills, knowledge, and beliefs that enable a person to engage in goal directed, self-regulated, autonomous behavior. Self-determination is an understanding of one's strengths and limitations together with a belief in oneself as capable and effective. When acting on the basis of these skills and attitudes, individuals have a greater ability to take control of their lives and assume the roles of adults in our society. (Field, Martin, Miller, Ward, & Wehmeyer, 1998b)

An individual's ability to achieve success and improve his or her quality of life as an adult is in direct relationship to the individual's level of self-determination. While much of the literature on self-determination focuses on involvement in the IEP process, students and their families must also be prepared to apply these skills in all settings (employment, postsecondary education, independent living, community involvement, and personal-social relationships) in which an adult is expected to function (Halpern, 1994).

STUDENT INVOLVEMENT ON THE ASSESSMENT TEAM

Transition assessment is most meaningful when it relates the personal attributes of the student to the demands of the environment in which the student will function in the near or distant future. Miller et al. (2007) identified eight future environments in which a student will need to exhibit self-determined behavior. These environments include the following: recreation and leisure, community participation, living arrangements, mobility and transportation, health care, agency supports, daily living skills, and financial management. Designing assessment approaches based on the student's expressed vision serves as the cornerstone of student empowerment and self-determination. Students with disabilities should be presented the opportunity to make choices in school and out of school settings, and their families can provide assistance by helping to establish future goals.

The transition assessment process must be structured so students with disabilities and/or their families can become active participants on the assessment team. Students and/or their families need to have input as to what will be assessed and what data-gathering methods will be utilized by the team. This can be accomplished, in part, by basing assessment activities on the student's and/or family's vision for the future. Once the vision is known, the questions that need to be addressed through assessment procedures can be developed. The following case studies illustrate questions that can help turn a student's vision for the future into a reality.

Case Study 1

Suzanne, a junior in high school, had a vision of becoming a veterinary technician, getting her own apartment within two years of high school graduation, and purchasing a car. Suzanne's teacher helped her brainstorm the steps it would take to accomplish her vision. Assessment questions generated during the brainstorming session included the following:

- What skills will I need to succeed in the veterinary technician program?
- What skills do I need to live on my own?
- What skills do I need to purchase and own a car?
- What skills do I have to succeed in the veterinary technician program?
- What skills do I have to live on my own?
- What skills do I have to purchase and own a car?
- What skills will I need to learn in order to succeed in the veterinary technician program?
- What skills do I need to develop to live on my own?
- What skills do I need to develop to purchase and own a car?
- What support services will I need to succeed in the veterinary technician program?
- What support services will I need to live on my own?
- What support services do I need to purchase and own a car?

Suzanne identified a nearby community college that offered a two-year certificate program in her career interest area. She then contacted the college to determine what the entrance requirements were. With respect to independent living, Suzanne decided that she and her parents needed to fill out an informal checklist that assisted her in identifying the daily living skills she would need to live on her own. With help from her teacher, she designed an informal assessment strategy to measure her ability to budget money. As a result, Suzanne researched and determined the typical wages of a veterinary technician, listed her fixed monthly expenses, and then designed a budget based on this information. Suzanne and her teacher also wanted to know whether Suzanne was prepared to be a self-advocate. To resolve that issue, they designed a list of interview questions that Suzanne could use with her family and other teachers to determine which, if any, self-advocacy skills she needed to develop prior to attending the community college.

Once the assessment data were collected, Suzanne's teacher assisted her in interpreting the results. As a result of academic testing, she found that her current academic skills needed some improvement over the next year. She also learned that her learning disability in the area of written language was still significant. This would qualify her for support services while attending the community college. A review of the daily living checklist revealed that laundry and basic home maintenance were skills that needed further attention. During the financial-budgeting exercise, Suzanne ran out of money about halfway between pay periods. Additional instruction in this area was clearly needed. Although Suzanne exhibited a number of self-advocacy skills as indicated by interviewing her family and teachers, it was felt that she had difficulty asking for help when she needed it, was not too familiar with community resources, and knew very little about her legal rights. Suzanne and her teacher developed a list of goals and strategies for improving her skills in each of these areas.

In the preceding case study, the student was directly involved in various phases of transition assessment. The student expressed her interests, preferences, and abilities; she assisted in the development of assessment methods and questions; she conducted some of the data-gathering activities; and she worked with the teacher in developing goals and strategies in response to the assessment results. It is likely that this student will assume greater responsibility for obtaining the skills necessary to be successful and independent in the adult world.

Case Study 2

Brian lived with his family and had a job supported by a job coach in the community. He had turned 18 this year, and his transition specialist and family agreed that they needed to meet to refine the plan for his transition from school to adult roles. Brian indicated through his communication board that he would like to participate in the planning meeting. His transition specialist asked Brian and his parents to indicate who should attend the meeting. His parents and transition specialist generated a list of potential participants, and Brian indicated through a yes/no response those persons he wanted to include. He also added two of his friends.

A meeting was held that included Brian's parents, his sister, his special education teacher, one of his general education teachers, his job coach, the transition specialist, and two of his friends. The purpose of the meeting was to establish a vision for Brian's future related to employment, postsecondary education, independent living, community involvement, and personal-social relationships. The consensus of the group was that Brian really enjoyed working as a copy clerk assistant. He hoped he would not have to go to school again in the near future. He wanted to eventually move into an apartment and attend sporting events, movies, and concerts. He hoped to maintain his friendships with the other young men in his Circle of Friends group. The transition specialist generated a list of assessment questions related to the vision established during this meeting. The questions included the following:

- What skills are needed to succeed as a copy clerk assistant, live on one's own, attend spectator events in the community, and maintain friendships?
- What skills did Brian have relevant to employment as a copy clerk assistant, living on his own, attending spectator events in the community, and maintaining friendships?
- What were the missing pieces that Brian needed in order to be successful at work, in an apartment, during spectator events, and in maintaining friendships?
- What skills was Brian likely to learn in his last three years of education that would be related to his goals?
- What support services was Brian going to need to be able to be successful in his future environments?

The participants in the planning meeting brainstormed a list of skills that were most likely needed to succeed as a copy clerk assistant; to live in an apartment; to attend sporting events, movies, and concerts; and to maintain friendships. Brian's transition specialist offered to validate the list by meeting with someone who supervises copy clerk assistants. Brian's special education teacher volunteered to meet with the supervisor of a supported living program in the community to validate the independent living list. Brian's parents asked to meet with an occupational and recreational therapist to validate the list of skills for spectator events. Brian's friends volunteered to talk to other friends to determine what skills are needed to maintain friendships. The group then agreed to get together again to discuss their findings and plan how to assess Brian's skills related to these areas.

A second meeting was held in which each modified list of skills was presented and the group, including Brian, rated Brian on the skills. Brian had several skills in each area along with some needs. The group then talked about which need areas could be translated into educational objectives and which needs would require ongoing support. From this list, an IEP and a list of potential agency linkages was generated.

ASSESSING AND DEVELOPING SELF-DETERMINATION SKILLS

As indicated earlier in this chapter, students with disabilities must be prepared to assume greater responsibility for developing, implementing, and evaluating the transition goals and objectives that are written into IEPs. Evaluating the student's readiness to assume this role is an important function of transition assessment activities. Moreover, transition assessment should generate a record of student self-determination skills exhibited during the IEP meeting, as well as a record of the student's level of independence in carrying out IEP goals and objectives.

Self-Determined IEP Assessment

The assessment process can be broken down into the three stages of IEP preparation, IEP performance, and IEP implementation (see Figure 3.1).

For students with disabilities to be active participants in the IEP meeting, a number of premeeting activities should be undertaken to ensure that the students have been adequately prepared for their role in the process. The importance of assessing students' readiness to participate in the IEP meeting cannot be overstated. If the answer to any of the assessment questions is no, additional instruction should take place to ensure that the student is adequately prepared for this very important event.

Once students with disabilities have been prepared to participate in the IEP meeting, they are ready to become active players on the IEP team. The intent is to have students fully participate in all phases of discussion related to their educational planning. The focus of assessment questions is

Figure 3.1   Assessing IEP Self-Determination Skills

IEP Preparation

1. Does the student understand the purpose of the IEP meeting?
2. Can the student explain the law guaranteeing his or her rights and requiring the IEP?
3. Does the student know who will be attending the IEP meeting?
4. Whom does the student want to invite to the IEP meeting?
5. Does the student know what roles the IEP participants will play?
6. Has the student reviewed current assessment information?
7. Has the student developed a list of personal goals to share at the meeting?
8. Has the student developed a list of questions to ask at the meeting?
9. Has the student practiced expressing his or her interests, preferences, and strengths?
10. Is the student prepared to ask for instructional and/or curriculum accommodations?

IEP Performance

1. Did the student know who was in attendance at the IEP meeting and their roles?
2. Was the student able to express his or her interests, preferences, and abilities?
3. Did the student express his or her personal goals and aspirations?
4. Did the student ask relevant questions?
5. Did the student request appropriate accommodations (if needed)?
6. Did the student express personal responsibility for goal seeking and attainment?
7. Did the student facilitate or co-facilitate the IEP meeting?
8. Is the student satisfied with the IEP meeting outcomes/results?
9. What does the student think could have been done to improve the meeting?

IEP Implementation

1. Does the student attend class on time?
2. Does the student request instructional support when needed?
3. Does the student request testing accommodations when needed?
4. Does the student assume responsibility for successes and failures?
5. Is the student aware of and working toward IEP goals?
6. Does the student believe he or she is receiving the support needed to reach IEP goals?
7. Has the student explored postsecondary options and support services?
8. Can the student explain which postsecondary options match his or her goals and needs?
9. Has the student developed a plan and timeline for contacting adult service providers?

---

now oriented toward the level of self-determined behavior exhibited during the IEP meeting itself.

After the IEP meeting has concluded, the assessment team evaluates the extent of student ownership for implementing IEP goals and objectives. As a result of self-determination activities, students with disabilities should have a greater understanding of their individual roles in implementing the goals, objectives, and activities of the IEP. At this stage, transition assessment team members need to monitor the extent to which students independently carry out the activities prescribed within the IEP.

Assessing student preparation to participate in the IEP process, observing student behavior during the IEP meeting, and evaluating the extent to which students are implementing IEP goals and objectives are each important transition assessment activities. Although the IEP process is only one forum where students with disabilities can demonstrate self-determination skills, it does provide a valuable context for assessing student readiness to initiate self-determined behavior in multiple settings both within and outside the educational setting.

Self-Determination Strategies and Curricula

A number of strategies and curricula are available that teachers and families can use to assist students with disabilities to become more self-determined and to apply these skills to the transition planning and IEP process (Field, Martin, Miller, Ward, & Wehmeyer, 1998a). The selection of a particular strategy should depend on the student's ability to communicate his or her interests and needs through the transition assessment process.

ChoiceMaker Self-Determination Curriculum

Increasing student participation in the IEP process is a fundamental goal of the *ChoiceMaker Curriculum* (Martin et al., 1997), formerly known as the Self-Directed IEP. This curriculum is an 11-step process that promotes the active participation and/or facilitation of the IEP meeting by individual students with disabilities. After receiving direct instruction on each of the 11 steps in the process, students are encouraged to assume a central role during the IEP meeting. The active participation of students during the IEP meeting will increase the likelihood that their expressed interests and goals are taken into serious consideration by the entire IEP team. It is also projected that students who actively participate in developing IEP goals and objectives will assume greater responsibility for implementing them. Assessment activities that could be used in conjunction with the *ChoiceMaker Curriculum* include the following: (a) direct observation of students during the IEP meeting, (b) student self-reports of IEP performance, (c) direct observation of student initiation of IEP goals and objectives, and (d) self-reports of student-initiated IEP goals and objectives.

Figure 3.2   Steps in the FUTURE Planning Strategy

The strategy is based upon a mnemonic device whereby each letter stands for a step of the strategy. This will help the student remember the steps to the strategy by simply remembering the word.

Step 1: **F—Find facts** about yourself related to
- Your strengths
- Areas you would like to improve
- Your disability
- Your legal rights
- Community resources
- Post–high-school education options
- Employment options
- Other adult roles

Step 2: **U—Understand and value** your
- Dreams
- Unique differences
- Rights
- Ability to take care of yourself

Step 3: **T—Think what is required and tell what is needed** to achieve the goals you have set for yourself for life after high school as a
- Worker
- Family member
- Community member
- Consumer
- Postsecondary student
- Other adult roles

Step 4: **U—Use the information to make a plan** that lays out the steps for achieving the goals you have set for yourself for life after high school.

Step 5: **R—Reach your goals** through your plan by
- Using community resources
- Following through on planned actions
- Asking for reasonable accommodations along the way

Step 6: **E—Evaluate the outcome** of the plan:
- Compare outcomes with expectations
- Celebrate success
- Adjust the plan if needed
- Develop a new plan

SOURCE: Begun, (1995, p. 53).

FUTURE Strategy

Begun (1995) has developed a strategy to prepare students for participation in the transition-planning process. The strategy contains six steps that lead to student-directed planning (see Figure 3.2).

The strategy title, an acronym using the beginning letter of each step, is "FUTURE." The F stands for "Find facts" about self. This first step toward self-determination includes all of the transition assessment activities the student and the IEP team undertake. The U represents "Understanding self." This step involves the interpretation of assessment results in personal terms. Ability-based results will assist in the development of self-esteem through learning to value one's unique set of experiences, strengths, and accomplishments. The T stands for "Think" about what is required in one's future. This step refers to an analysis of the demands of desired postsecondary settings. This may also include essential functions of a job or entry-level requirements of a training program. "Using the information" is the next step in the process. Here the student is asked to use the information to develop transition plans based on the IEP. The plan must be built on the student's knowledge of self, the knowledge of the desired outcomes, and a true synthesis of this information as indicated by the student's acceptance of his or her uniqueness. "R" represents "Reach your goals." This procedure includes carrying out IEP activities and reaching the student's goals. The last step, "Evaluate the outcome," refers to all evaluation of student progress toward goals and the making of any adjustments necessary to reach the desired outcomes.

This strategy may be used independently with students with mild disabilities. For students with more severe disabilities, the strategy could serve as a guide for the transition assessment and planning process and should be used by the person facilitating the assessment and planning process.

Next S.T.E.P

The *Next S.T.E.P.* curriculum (Halpern, Herr, Doren, & Wolf, 2000) is a set of lessons that will help students plan for the future. It uses an approach that will assist students in taking charge of developing a transition plan for leaving school and beginning to live as adults in the community. The goals of this curriculum are to help students to (a) become motivated to engage in transition planning, (b) engage in meaningful and useful self-evaluation, (c) identify and select feasible and personally desired transition goals and activities, (d) monitor the implementation of their transition plans and make adjustments when needed, and (e) take responsibility for conducting their own transition-planning meeting.

The Self-Advocacy Strategy

Another popular model for increasing and assessing student participation in the IEP process is The Self-Advocacy Strategy, formerly known as the I PLAN Strategy (Van Reusen, Bos, Schumaker, & Deshler, 1994). The Self-Advocacy Strategy is a seven-step procedure that is designed to promote effective planning and communication for students during their IEP meetings. Like the Self-Directed IEP model discussed earlier, the Self-Advocacy Strategy approach should be taught to students with disabilities in advance of the IEP meeting. An important component of the Self-Advocacy Strategy is the I-PLAN Strategy, which is used to develop the actual IEP. Specific questions that are asked to assess students implementing the Self-Advocacy Strategy through the IEP include the following:

- Did the student **Inventory** his or her strengths, weaknesses, goals, and interests?
- Did the student **Provide** his or her inventory information?
- Did the student **Listen** and respond during the meeting?
- Did the student **Ask** questions during the meeting?
- Did the student **Name** his or her goals?

Like the Self-Directed IEP approach, the Self-Advocacy Strategy provides transition assessment personnel with an important context for determining student readiness to exhibit self-determination skills in future IEP meetings and in related community, work, and home settings.

STEPS TO SELF-DETERMINATION

The *Steps to Self-Determination* curriculum (Hoffman & Field, 2005) was developed for students in middle and high school programs. Its purpose is to help adolescents with and without disabilities become more self-determined. There are detailed lesson plans for each session. *Steps to Self-Determination* can be used in the general education or special education classroom and by school and rehabilitation counselors and family support groups.

Instruments for Assessing Self-Determination

There are a number of formal and informal tools for assessing the self-determination skills of youth with and without disabilities. Some of these instruments are sold by themselves, some are affiliated with the curricula described in the previous section (but can be used separately from those curricula), and some can be used only in conjunction with specific curricula.

AIR Self-Determination Scale and User Guide

The purpose of the *AIR Self-Determination Scale* (Wolman, Campeau, DuBois, Mithaug, & Stolarski, 1994) is to help educators prepare student-age youth with disabilities to demonstrate self-actualization, self-determination, and independence. The scale uses four different forms: the educator form, student form, parent form, and research form. Each of the forms has similar but different questions. All forms utilize a rating scale from 1 (*never*) to 5 (*always*), with the last page allowing the individual to write out short answers to a few questions.

The Arc's Self-Determination Scale

The *Arc's Self-Determination Scale* (Wehmeyer, 2000) takes between 30 minutes and one hour to complete and was created to assist adolescents with cognitive disabilities (mild cognitive, mild mental retardation, and learning disabilities) to recognize their strengths and weaknesses in the area of self-determination through the use of a self-report measure. The scale includes 72 items and consists of four parts: autonomy, self-regulation, psychological empowerment, and self-realization—all of which the Arc deems essential components of self-determination. The first section, on autonomy, asks students to check the answer that best describes them in given situations. Section two, self-regulation, offers the students several stories which consist of a beginning and an end; the student then is asked to fill in the best answer to complete the story. Psychological empowerment and self-realization, sections three and four, ask the students to check the answer that best describes them. If needed, the test can be read orally to ensure that the student understands the concepts; a teacher or others may also transcribe the written section for the students if needed. Scoring procedures include a point system that varies, depending on the section. The raw scores are collected for each section and a final score is then calculated.

ChoiceMaker Self-Determination Curriculum:
Take Action and *ChoiceMaker Self-Determination Assessment*

The *ChoiceMaker Self-Determination Curriculum: Take Action* includes an instructional video along with seven lessons designed to help students assess, develop, and implement their goals. Included in this program is the *ChoiceMaker Self-Determination Assessment*. This assessment instrument includes a pretest and posttest tool that determines a student's level of self-determination before and after participating in the ChoiceMaker Curriculum. The pre-assessment indicates the specific self-determination skills the student currently possesses and indicates the skills that need to be developed. The post-assessment tool indicates what skills were attained as a result of participation in the *ChoiceMaker Self-Determination Curriculum*.

Next S.T.E.P. Transition Skills Inventory

The Transition Skills Inventory (TSI) is an assessment component built within the self-evaluation unit of the *Next S.T.E.P.* curriculum (Halpern et al., 2000). The TSI is a rating scale used to evaluate the student's strengths and weaknesses in the four areas of personal life, jobs, education and training, and living on one's own. There is a lesson to introduce the TSI to the students so they learn how to rate themselves and about the process of self-evaluation. The students complete the TSI in the workbooks that follow the curriculum being used. It is stressed to the students that the TSI is not a test and how important it is to be honest when completing it. The TSI is designed for the students to use their own ratings and the ratings of their teachers and support personnel to complete the TSI profile report.

Self-Determination Assessment Battery

The *Self-Determination Assessment Battery* (Hoffman, Field, & Sawilowsky, 2004) was designed to measure cognitive, affective, and behavioral factors related to self-determination. This assessment uses five different instruments: Self-Determination Knowledge Scale (SDKS) Pretest, forms A & B; Self-Determination Parent Perceptions Scale (PPS); Self-Determination Teacher Perception Scale (TPS); Self-Determination Observation Checklist (SDOC); and Self-Determination Student Scale (SDSS). The authors hope to promote an emphasis on involvement and self-determination by giving students, parents, and teachers feedback on progress related to skills and knowledge for self-determination. The battery is designed for individuals with mild to moderate disabilities who are age 14 and above.

Self-Determination and Self-Advocacy Skills Questionnaire

A set of tools that can be utilized to assess students' level of self-determination was recently developed by Miller et al. (2007). The Self-Determination and Self-Advocacy Skills Questionnaire consists of five forms including the following: Student Form, Parent Form, Educator Form, Student and Teacher Interview: Performance Battery, and Scoring Summary Sheet. By collecting information from the student, parents, and educators, the assessment team will be able to determine if self-determination skills are being exhibited in school, community, and home environments. These tools will also enable the assessment team to determine if the perceptions of the student, parent(s), and teachers are in agreement with respect to the student's self-determination and self-advocacy skills.

Futures Planning Inventory

Miller et al. (2007) also developed an instrument that can be utilized to assist students with disabilities to plan for their future after high school. The Future Planning Inventory examines postsecondary options such as education including four-year colleges, universities, community colleges, and technical colleges. In addition, postschool employment, independent living, recreation and leisure, transportation, financial, and health-related options are indicated on the inventory. In order to gather perspectives from teachers and parents, additional forms of the instrument have been developed. Form 1 is to be completed by the student. Form 2 is to be completed by the parent/guardian, and Form 3 is to be completed by a teacher.

SUMMARY

A fundamental purpose of self-determination is to promote student independence within school, community, work, and home settings. The assessment of the student's self-determination skills is critical to determining what additional instruction and experiences in self-determination the student needs. Students who are able to assume greater responsibility for their actions, academic or otherwise, will stand a much better chance of experiencing the intrinsic rewards that come with increased levels of independence.

The self-determination initiative represents another major paradigm shift within the field of special education. Until recently, students with disabilities seldom played a significant role in the development, implementation, or evaluation of their own educational goals. Transition assessment that is based on the principle of self-determination will enable the IEP team to create an outcome-oriented document that reflects the personal goals and aspirations of individual students. The long-term intent of self-determination assessment and planning is to ensure that students with disabilities are capable of making decisions throughout adulthood that are based on what they know to be true about their strengths, needs, preferences, and interests.

REFERENCES

Begun, W. H. (1995). The FUTURE strategy. In W. H. Begun, L. Minor, B. Silvers, & P. Witcher (Eds.), *The TRANS-PLAN curriculum* (pp. 52–53). Desoto, KS: Desoto School District.

Field, S., Martin, J., Miller, R., Ward, M., & Wehmeyer, M. (1998a). *A practical guide to teaching self-determination* . Reston, VA: Council for Exceptional Children.

Field, S., Martin, J., Miller, R., Ward, M. & Wehmeyer, M. (1998b). Self-determination for persons with disabilities: A position statement of the Division on Career Development and Transition, Council for Exceptional Children. *Career Development for Exceptional Individuals, 21*(2), 113–128.

Halpern, A. S. (1994). The transition of youth with disabilities to adult life: A position statement of the Division on Career Development and Transition. *Career Development for Exceptional Individuals, 17*, 115–124.

Halpern, A. S., Herr, C. M., Doren, B., & Wolf, N. H. (2000). *Next S.T.E.P.: Student transition and educational planning* (2nd ed.). Austin, TX: PRO-ED.

Hoffman, A., & Field, S. (2005). *Steps to self-determination: A curriculum to help adolescents learn to achieve their goals* (2nd ed.). Austin, TX: PRO-ED.

Hoffman, A., Field, S., Sawilowsky, S. (2004). *Self-determination assessment battery and user's guide* (3rd ed.). Detroit, MI: Wayne State University Center for Self-Determination and Transition.

Individuals with Disabilities Education Act, U.S.C. § 1401 (1990).

Individuals with Disabilities Education Act Amendments of 1997, 20 U.S.C. § 1400 (1997).

Individuals with Disabilities Education Improvement Act of 2004, 20 U.S.C. § 1400 (2004).

Martin, J. E., Marshall, L. H., Maxson, L., Jerman, P., Hughes, W., Miller, T., & McGill, T. (1997). *ChoiceMaker instructional series.* Longmont, CO: Sopris West.

Miller, R. J., Lombard, R. C., & Corbey, S. A. (2007). *Transition assessment: Planning transition and IEP development for youth with mild to moderate disabilities.* Boston: Allyn & Bacon.

Mithaug, D. E. (1993). *To choose or not to choose.* Paper presented at the First Annual Kansas Systems Change Statewide Conference, Salina.

Test, D., Mason, C., Hughes, C., Konrad, M., Melia, N., & Wood, W. (2004). Student involvement in individualized education program meetings. *Exceptional Children, 70,* 391–412.

Van Reusen, A. K., Bos, C. S., Schumaker, J. B., & Deshler, D. D. (1994). *The self advocacy strategy for education and transition planning.* Lawrence, KS: Edge.

Wehmeyer, M. D. (1996). Self-determination as an educational outcome: Why is it important to children, youth, and adults with disabilities? In D. J. Sands & M. L. Wehmeyer (Eds.), *Self-determination across the life span: Independence and choice for people with disabilities* (pp. 15–34). Baltimore: Paul H. Brooks.

Wehmeyer, M. L. (2000). *The Arc's self-determination scale: Procedural guidelines* (Revised). Silver Spring, MD: The Arc of the United States.

Wehmeyer, M. L., & Schwartz, M. (1998). The self-determination focus of transition goals for students with mental retardation. *Career Development for Exceptional Individuals, 21,* 75–86.

Wolman, J. M., Campeau, P. L., DuBois, P. A., Mithaug, D. E., & Stolarski, V. S. (1994). *AIR self-determination scale and user guide.* Palo Alto, CA: American Institutes for Research.

4

Using Outcomes of Assessment for IEP Planning

This chapter provides the rationale and strategies for using transition assessment in individualized education program (IEP) planning. The purpose of this chapter is to

- Discuss how to integrate transition assessment into all parts of the IEP and IEP process, as outlined in the Individuals with Disabilities Education Improvement Act of 2004 (IDEA 2004)
- Provide case studies to illustrate this integration
- Provide a sample set of IEP goals and objectives (as appropriate) related to transition planning in the five areas identified by Halpern (1994)

INTEGRATING TRANSITION ASSESSMENT INTO THE IEP

As discussed in Chapter 1, IDEA 2004 contains specific provisions related to transition assessment and the development of an IEP. It clearly mandates transition assessment as the basis for the transition services that are included in the IEP. The legislation specifies the need for measurable postsecondary goals that are based on "appropriate transition assessment." Furthermore, IDEA 2004 expands the definition of the statement of the student's present level of educational performance to include a statement of both academic and *functional* performance. IDEA 2004 also continues the requirement for a statement of transition services for all students age 16 and above (and younger if appropriate). This statement must include the student's course of study and the services necessary to achieve the student's measurable post-secondary objectives. In addition, IDEA 2004 mandates that the student must be invited to the IEP meeting when transition-related issues are to be addressed. When the student cannot attend, the school must take other steps to ensure that the student's preferences and interests are considered. All of the IDEA 2004 provisions highlighted above underscore the need for transition assessment to occur prior to the development of an IEP. This assessment is the baseline from which to design services and to measure progress toward desired postsecondary outcomes. Transition assessment is the foundation upon which the transition components of the IEP are developed.

The transition language in IDEA 2004 challenges the IEP team to infuse transition planning throughout the IEP in the areas of training, education, employment, and independent living skills. IDEA 2004 charges schools to use the IEP as the vehicle for planning for anticipated individual student needs beyond the completion of secondary education. This mandate significantly shifts the focus of the IEP from the narrow view of planning for interventions to support the student within the school to the broader vision of preparing the student for roles beyond school.

Traditionally, IEP teams design programming for one year at a time, but transition programming often requires longer-range planning. The inclusion of transition planning in the IEP should prompt special educators to consider each IEP as an intermediary plan that consecutively leads to the achievement of long-range goals. Thus, IDEA 2004 requires a shift in focus for the IEP that is not only school-focused but adds postsecondary outcomes to the mix.

The focus on transition planning and services has caused special educators to reshape the individualized education planning process. This transformation has moved the focus from inside the school walls to the world beyond. While the value of this major change cannot be disputed for students with disabilities, the obligation for carrying out this shift has clearly been placed upon the local school district. It is only natural for special educators to have questions and concerns related to fulfilling this obligation.

WHAT IS THE FIRST STEP IN TRANSITION PLANNING USING THE IEP?

While the IEP is the primary tool for establishing an annual educational plan, transition planning requires a multistep process. The process begins by asking the student to define his or her vision for the future. In our educational system, students are seldom asked this type of question and may have difficulty addressing these future-oriented issues. Many students cannot define their strengths and challenges or list reasonable accommodations necessary to ensure success. Other students may not be allowed to make even the simplest decisions that affect their day-to-day lives. Many students served through special education are perceived by professionals as being unrealistic. Often when students share their dreams, with the best of intentions, staff feel compelled to reel in their fantasies. This cuts off any chance of further dialogue and exploration of the wide array of future options. Students are sometimes perceived as unmotivated which leads to staff talking "around" them and asking future-directed questions to parents and family members. Some students are not considered integral members of their IEP teams by either special education professionals or their families. For students to fully realize their potential and become the integral part of the IEP team mandated by the IDEA 2004 legislation, they must be encouraged to develop and use self-determination skills (see Chapter 3).

Once the student has established a vision for the future, he or she works with the team to assess skills and interests in light of the demands of the desired future living, working, and educational environments. This assessment should reveal the student's present level of functioning as compared to what will be needed in the envisioned future. Thus the assessment is tailored to the student's desired outcomes and provides the foundation for transition planning and service needs that are addressed through the IEP. These needs, preferences, and interests should be identified through comprehensive transition assessment that addresses all the areas of anticipated adult roles. The results of the assessment should subsequently be infused into the IEP.

HOW ARE THE RESULTS OF TRANSITION ASSESSMENT INFUSED INTO THE PRESENT LEVEL OF ACADEMIC ACHIEVEMENT AND FUNCTIONAL PERFORMANCE?

The present level of performance statement must accurately describe the student's performance in both academic and functional areas. In addition to academic assessment, assessment results based on the student's desired interests and preferences, such as the requisite skills for a specific job, independent living, community involvement, personal/social relationships, and the ability to self-advocate, should be reported. The present level of performance statement highlights the student's functioning level at the present time and leads to the clarification of student needs. The statement serves as the foundation for the service plan delineated through the IEP.

The present level of performance statement should be written in objective, measurable terms. An example of a statement found in the present level of performance statement might be that "the student independently uses public transportation regularly to go to and from work and social events." This statement is based on informal information but is critical to assessing the student's mobility within the community. Data reported in the present level of performance statement may be based on informal measures, which are usually more functionally descriptive than standardized test results. Test scores from formal assessment measures may be reported in the present level of performance statement but should be self-explanatory or presented in functional terms. For example, results of formal aptitude assessment could be included in the statement. However, simply reporting percentile ranking on specific aptitudes means little without an explanation of the relationship this specific aptitude profile has to possible career aspirations. A student who scores in the 20th percentile on spatial relations on a standardized aptitude assessment may have a difficult time succeeding as an architect. The present level of performance statement describing this assessment result could be, "Cathy does not have a realistic view of the demands of her desired career field and needs to carry out further career exploration activities to determine whether her aptitude profile (20th percentile in spatial relations on the aptitude assessment) is a good match with the requirements of her desired career (architect)." This statement presents a standardized score, but puts it in the context of the demands of a career area and desired outcomes.

HOW ARE THE RESULTS OF TRANSITION ASSESSMENT USED IN IEP PLANNING?

Upon completion of the present level of performance statement, the IEP team must develop a plan for the specially designed instruction and related services to be offered to the student. Although IEP formats differ markedly among school districts, each need area identified in the present level of performance statement must be addressed within the subsequent sections of the IEP. The content of the IEP is mandated by the IDEA 2004 legislation and includes academic and functional goals; a statement of special education, related services, and supplementary aids and services; accommodations that are necessary to assess and support the student; and a statement of postsecondary goals and transition services. It should be noted that IDEA 2004 eliminated the requirement that all special education students must have short-term goals and/or benchmarks. Only students who are taking alternate assessment that is aligned to alternate standards must have short-term objectives and or benchmarks included in their IEPs.

Although each identified need must be addressed, there may be multiple ways to address each need through the IEP. Some confusion exists about how to address challenges that are identified through transition assessment and found in the present level of performance statement. Areas of need delineated in the present level of performance statement that require instruction and student achievement over time should be addressed through annual goals and, if appropriate, short-term objectives. Annual goals should reflect student growth. For example, through assessment it is revealed that a student cannot use units of measurement. The student wants to become a cosmetologist. His future setting demands include accurate measurement of chemicals. His IEP team should generate an annual goal related to the development of relevant measurement skills for this student.

Not all transition needs require annual goals. Some transition need areas listed in the present level of performance statement can be addressed with "one-shot" activities and are not appropriate content for goals. For example, a student may want to contact the local vocational school to determine enrollment procedures and entrance requirements. This is a one-time activity, does not usually require instruction, and does not involve measurable intermediary steps to arrive at mastery. It is not an appropriate activity for the annual goals section of the IEP. Depending on the custom in the individual state or school district, this activity could be listed elsewhere, such as in notes from the IEP meeting, or even in the statement of transition service section.

Another example of a need that does not require formal instructional services may require an agency linkage. A student wants to attend a community college but cannot afford tuition. The transition service that should be delineated on the IEP would be for "the student to contact the financial aid officer at the community college and a vocational rehabilitation counselor to determine the availability of financial support." Thus, the IEP would specify agency linkages to meet the student's need.

WHAT ABOUT INTERAGENCY LINKAGES?

An additional provision of IDEA requires that schools develop interagency linkages with adult service agencies that can serve students with disabilities as they leave the educational system and make their transition to adult roles. This need for interagency collaboration reflects the realization that students cannot be totally prepared to assume their adult roles upon completion of their public school education and may continue to require support as their adult roles emerge. The need for the linkages that will provide support to the young adult should be identified through the transition assessment process. The actual interagency linkages and services to be provided should be outlined in the statement of transition services. For example, a student is planning to attend the local community technical college. Through transition assessment, it is determined that the student will need assistance in asking for accommodations from his college teachers. To address this concern, he will work with the disability support office at the community college. As mandated by IDEA, a representative from the community college should be invited to attend the IEP meeting. The services that will be provided through the community college should be included in the statement of transition services in the IEP. Another example of the need for agency linkages might be a student who needs a supported living arrangement after graduation. For this student, a representative from the Developmental Disabilities Association could be invited to the meeting to discuss community housing options.

Case Studies

Guidelines on how to write a statement of needed transition services and formats vary from state to state. The case studies that follow represent some examples of how the concepts presented in this chapter can be applied. These cases include the statement of transition services written in narrative form, as well as examples of both formal and informal transition assessment. Sample transition goals and objectives (when appropriate) are included with each of the case studies.

(text continues on p. 59)

How Do I Apply These Concepts to a College-Bound Student With Mild Disabilities?

Student History

Matt always knew that he would go to college. All of his brothers and sisters were going. Why shouldn't he? When Matt was nine years old, he was identified as having a learning disability and was served through a special education resource room 2 hours a day in the areas of reading, writing, and spelling. He really did not like being pulled out of class to go to another room.

Transition Assessment

When Matt got to high school, his special education teacher asked him to talk about what he wanted to do when he graduated from high school. It was difficult for Matt to share his vision, because no one had ever asked him what he wanted to do. He told his teacher that he wanted to go to college, but he did not have a specific career choice. His teacher talked to him about the benefits of transition planning and the need to start as a freshman getting ready for life after high school. He and his teacher began to plan his transition assessment. Together they decided that Matt would need to be able to self-advocate if he were to be successful in college. Matt thought he was a good self-advocate, but he agreed to ask his physical science teacher for classroom and testing accommodations. He would then ask the physical science teacher to evaluate his ability to self-advocate using an informal checklist that he and his teacher developed. Matt also wanted information related to his current academic functioning. He agreed to do a writing sample as well as take subtests of an achievement test related to reading, writing, and spelling. Matt's teacher also wanted him to tape-record an informal interview in which he and his family reviewed his functional living skills and awareness of adult services. Because Matt was not sure what he wanted to major in during college, he agreed to take a computer-based interest inventory.

Assessment Results

Matt was surprised to find out that he had some problems with self-advocacy. He could not describe what accommodations he needed to be successful in physical science. He also had difficulty talking to his physical science teacher about his disability. On the achievement test, Matt scored below grade level on reading, written language, and spelling. He was able to identify three areas of interest on his interest assessment. Both he and his parents described his independent living skills as adequate. Neither Matt nor his parents were aware of any adult service agencies that could assist in Matt's transition. Matt was able to identify several careers he was interested in, but was not able to select just one area of interest. The results of the assessment were included in the present level of performance statement on the IEP.

Transition Planning

As he and his teacher discussed his present level of performance, Matt agreed that he needed to work on self-advocacy skills and admitted that asking for the accommodations he needed was harder than he had anticipated. He especially wanted to become more aware of classroom and test-taking modifications that would help him. He also wanted to understand his learning disability and be able to describe it to others without becoming embarrassed. His teacher suggested that he work on acquiring learning strategies through the learning center and apply the strategies to his mainstream classes. Matt also decided that he wanted to explore the career areas of engineering and law enforcement by interviewing persons in those careers. During his junior and senior years, Matt planned to enroll in a career exploration class through which he could job-shadow persons working in the career areas he was interested in. Matt's teacher suggested that he invite a college representative who provides support services to students with disabilities at the local community college and a vocational rehabilitation counselor to his IEP meeting to discuss the services they can provide for Matt as he makes his transition from high school.

Statement of Needed Transition Services

Prior to the IEP meeting, Matt and his teacher met to discuss his assessment results. Based on the results of Matt's assessment, he and his teacher developed the following statement:

Matt will continue his enrollment in college preparatory classes and will work to make passing grades in all of the classes required by the state colleges. He will

(Continued)

(Continued)

research the dates of college entrance exams and work with the counselor to assure that he has the accommodations he needs for these tests. Matt will work with his learning center teacher to develop self-advocacy skills, including the ability to ask for reasonable accommodations and the ability to describe his learning disability in functional terms. Matt will also work with the learning center teacher to learn and apply learning strategies to written assignments in his high school classes as preparation for college. He also needs to explore his areas of vocational interest by contacting members of the community who work in the fields of veterinary medicine, sports, and engineering. Matt also needs to contact a vocational rehabilitation counselor and a representative from the local community college and state four-year colleges to determine what services might be available to assist him in his transition from high school.

Annual Goals

Matt and his teacher developed annual goals for two of the areas of need identified in the statement of transition services. The areas of self-advocacy and learning strategies each had an annual goal.

- *Annual Goal:* Matt will demonstrate self-advocacy skills by meeting individually with each of his teachers to request reasonable accommodations in each of his classes.
- *Annual Goal:* Matt will apply two learning strategies related to written communication to 100% of his assignments in the regular classroom.

How Do I Apply These Concepts to a Student With Mild Disabilities Who Will Attend a Two-Year Technical School?

Student History

When Nicole was in eighth grade and preparing to enroll in high school, she was told about classes offered to juniors and seniors that involved art and jobs. It caught her attention because she always enjoyed art but had never thought about being able to work as an artist. Nicole was a sophomore in high school now, and her IEP meeting was 2 months away. Nicole was also working with her special education teacher and guidance counselor on her schedule for the next year. She wanted to enroll in a graphic arts class at the area vocational-technical school next year.

Transition Assessment

Nicole's special education teacher suggested that Nicole needed to think beyond high school to decide whether or not the graphic arts program fit into her overall plan. Her teacher asked her to do an informal assessment activity in which Nicole had to write down what she wanted to do immediately after high school five years later, and ten years after that. She also asked Nicole what her ideal job would be, where she wanted to live, and how much money she thought she would need to be able to afford the life style she desired. Her teacher suggested that Nicole complete some vocational interest and aptitude assessments. The teacher also contacted the graphic arts teacher and arranged a meeting so that Nicole and she could determine what skills Nicole would need to be successful in the graphic arts class. The special education teacher worked with the graphic arts teacher to develop a curriculum-based assessment checklist of skills Nicole would be expected to develop through the graphic arts class, in order to determine which skill development activities would require additional support or accommodations. The graphic arts teacher reminded Nicole that she needed to submit a portfolio of artwork before being admitted to the class. Nicole completed an informal transition survey that asked her to assess her own skills related to being able to live on her own. Nicole's foster parents completed the survey as well.

Assessment Results

When Nicole completed the activity that asked her what she wanted to do after high school, she indicated that she hoped to finish her training within two years after high school and begin working. By the fifth year out of high school, she wanted to have a full-time job and be living on her own. At the ten-year mark she hoped to be married and living in a house she and her husband owned in the town where she grew up. She knew that if she got married she and her husband would probably both have to work. She also completed interest and aptitude assessments. Both assessments revealed a good match between her stated interest and her assessed interests and aptitudes. Nicole asked her current art teacher to evaluate her skills on the CBVA checklist. She also asked her English teacher to complete the CBVA checklist. Her art teacher felt that Nicole needed extra time to complete assignments, needed to be more careful about the condition of her final work, and needed some work in measurement skills. She felt that, with accommodations, Nicole would have no trouble achieving the items on the checklist. Her English teacher felt that Nicole needed to be more organized and had some trouble translating thoughts to written work. Through the transition survey that Nicole and her foster parents completed, the areas that appeared to need work were budgeting and time management. The results of the assessment were included in the present level of performance statement on the IEP.

Transition Planning

From the results of her assessment, Nicole and her teacher concluded that the graphic arts program through the area vocational-technical school would be a good option for her. Nicole's life goals suggested that a tech prep two-plus-two program in the area of graphic arts would meet her long-range goals. Nicole had no information related to postsecondary options and needed to contact the local technical college to find out about the graphic arts program. Nicole would work with her

(Continued)

(Continued)

high school art teacher to determine reasonable accommodations in order for her to be successful. Her special education teacher suggested that Nicole work on organization and time-management strategies while in the special education resource room. She also suggested that Nicole review linear measurement skills. To strengthen her money-management skills, Nicole decided that she wanted to take a class called applied math, which teaches consumer skills and budgeting.

Statement of Needed Transition Services

Nicole's statement of needed transition services was developed based on her assessment results and planning. It read

Nicole will continue enrollment in a technical college preparatory curriculum and will take electives in the area of art. Nicole has identified the area of graphic arts as her career interest. She will work with her guidance counselor to apply for admission to the area vocational-technical program. Nicole will work with her high school art teacher to assemble a portfolio for submission at the time of application. Nicole has invited the admissions counselor and graphic arts teacher to attend her IEP meeting. She will also arrange a meeting with a representative from the local technical college to receive admission information for the postsecondary graphic arts program. Nicole needs to work on money-management skills in order to meet her goal of living independently. Through special education, Nicole will work on time-management and organization skills. She will also complete a review unit on linear measurement.

Annual Goals

The annual goals included in Nicole's IEP related to time-management and organization skills and measurement.

- *Annual Goal:* Nicole will complete an assignment log for each of her classes that lists all of her assignments and due dates, and indicate the date each assignment was turned in.
- *Annual Goal:* Nicole will demonstrate the use of linear measurement.

How Do I Apply These Concepts to a Student With Moderate Disabilities?

Student History

Jamey always liked to be around food. His mother let him help around the kitchen from the time he was five or six years old. When he went to high school, his favorite classes were always cooking classes. He sometimes needed help from his lab partners in measurement and in increasing or decreasing recipes. He was very good at preparing the ingredients and food presentation. When Jamey turned 16, his teacher began talking to him about what he wanted to do when he got out of school. Although Jamey knew he wanted to go to work someday, he was not really sure whether he wanted to be a chef. He only knew about the jobs he saw on television, and some of those looked pretty good. Jamey was not sure that he ever wanted to move out of his parents' house. He was comfortable there, and moving out scared him. He hoped to continue in Special Olympics so that he could stay in touch with his friends. His IEP meeting was one month away, and his teacher needed to determine Jamey's specific transition needs to be incorporated in the IEP.

Transition Assessment

Jamey's transition assessment was designed to determine his skills related to employment, independent living, community involvement, and knowledge of community resources. Jamey was asked to fill out an informal interest assessment with the help of the paraprofessional. Jamey's special education teacher asked his foods teacher to complete a checklist related to work behaviors and skills that Jamey demonstrated in the foods class. His special education teacher placed Jamey in a three-week situational assessment in the school cafeteria with a job coach to determine his level of work-related skills. His teacher sent home an informal transition checklist for Jamey's family to complete, which asked them to assess his present functioning related to daily living skills, self-help skills, community involvement, and knowledge of community resources. Jamey and his teacher filled out a copy of the same informal assessment.

Assessment Results

Jamey indicated a strong interest in food service but moderate interest in all other areas on the interest assessment. Jamey's foods teacher identified several areas of strengths and needs in his performance in the foods class. During Jamey's job sample in the cafeteria, the data collected by his job coach were consistent with his foods teacher's evaluation. Some additional observations were that Jamey became distracted easily, especially when learning new jobs, and that he did not ask for assistance when he did not know what to do. He also had a low production rate. However, his quality of work was excellent once he knew all of the steps in a task. On Jamey's transition survey, several areas of need were identified. Jamey's parents reported that he did no chores at home, including making his bed or caring for his own clothing. Jamey's mother stated that she felt it was easier to do the chores herself than to try to get Jamey to do them. Jamey seemed to manage his money well and had a savings account. He did not seem to know how much things cost, because his parents did all the shopping for him. Jamey's parents expressed their desire for Jamey to live on his own or in a supported living setting within the next five to ten years. They also reported that Jamey was quite active in the Special Olympics and used the public library frequently, but did little else outside of family activities. He rarely called friends from school and was content to sit in his room and play video games for hours at a time. Jamey's parents did not feel that either

(Continued)

(Continued)

Jamey or they had much knowledge about community resources. Jamey's survey responses were very similar to those of his parents. His teacher's form was consistent with both the parent and student forms. The results of the assessment were included in the present level of performance statement on the IEP.

Transition Planning

Although Jamey indicated a strong interest in food service, he and his teacher decided to do four three-week job samples in the community to try out several different jobs supervised on the work site by a job coach. During the job samples, Jamey would be asked to rate the quality of his work as well as how well he liked the job he was trying. At the end of the twelve-week period, Jamey would select the job on which he wanted to be placed with a job coach for paid employment.

Jamey did not seem to want to leave the safe environment of his parents' house and move into an independent living situation. Jamey had never visited any community living options. His teacher decided to arrange a field trip for her entire class to visit all of the supported living sites in the community. The question of whether Jamey could do daily chores was not resolved through the transition survey. Jamey's teacher suggested that Jamey and his parents contact the local independent living agency to request an evaluation of his independent living skills. She also suggested that they apply for housing this year, because there was at least a five-year waiting list for supported living apartments in the community.

When discussing the results of the survey, Jamey admitted that he would like to do things with friends and even have a girlfriend but did not know what to do for fun or how to invite friends to do things with him. His teacher suggested that she and Jamey go over the weekend section of the newspaper to look for events that he and a friend could attend. She also suggested that the class could role-play telephoning each other to ask for a date.

Jamey's teacher also saw the need to hold a meeting for the students in her class and their parents to inform them of the community agencies that could provide transition services. She invited agency representatives to talk to the group. From this meeting, she hoped that parents and students would contact appropriate agencies. She wanted to invite the local vocational rehabilitation counselor to Jamey's IEP meeting. After the parent meeting, both Jamey and his parents agreed that Vocational Rehabilitation could help with transition services for Jamey and should attend Jamey's IEP meeting.

Statement of Needed Transition Services

During Jamey's IEP meeting, the following statement of transition services was developed:

Jamey will continue his enrollment in general education classes with curricular modifications and support. He will continue to take electives in the area of food preparation and independent living. Jamey needs to explore several career options to affirm his interest in food service. He also needs to develop job skills through on-the-job training experiences in the community with a job coach. Jamey needs to explore community living options to build his level of confidence in his ability to live on his own. His functional living skills need to be assessed through a community living agency in a realistic setting. Jamey needs to complete an application for a supported living program and be put on a waiting list. He also needs to complete an application for services with Vocational Rehabilitation for transition support as he moves from high school to employment. Jamey also has social skills needs which will be addressed through instruction in his special education class. Another area to be addressed through instruction and community-based experiences is money management. Jamey does not know how much things cost and has no experience budgeting for expenditures.

Annual Goals

Jamey's teacher developed annual goals related to social skill development and money management.

- *Annual Goal:* Jamey will attend a school dance with a date.
- *Annual Goal:* Jamey will develop a budget based on his potential earnings and expenses.

How Do I Apply These Concepts to a Student With Severe Disabilities?

Student History

Nate is 18 years old. He lives with his parents and two sisters. Nate uses a communication board to express his basic needs and has some functional signs. He cannot understand abstract concepts. He uses a wheelchair for mobility. He has some acting-out behaviors when he is bored. He is patient with others who cannot understand his attempts to communicate. He has attended the neighborhood school since he was 12 years old and attends activities monthly with friends he made through a Circle of Friends program offered by his school. He participates in Special Olympics and enjoys being with age-appropriate peers. Nate has participated in some supported work experiences in the community and seems to enjoy productive activity. He likes to watch videos and has used some of the money he has earned to rent movies. He also likes to listen to music. Nate can feed himself but needs assistance toileting.

(Continued)

(Continued)

Transition Assessment

Nate's special education teacher organized a meeting with Nate and his family. After conferring with Nate and his family, she also invited Nate's neighbor, who provides respite care twice weekly, and one of the neighborhood peers who spends the most time with Nate. Nate's occupational, physical, and speech therapists also attended the meeting. Using a person-centered planning system, the teacher asked those who attended Nate's meeting what their dreams for Nate were, what their fears were, who Nate really was, his gifts, his needs, and what an ideal school day would be for Nate, especially related to readying him for making the transition from school to the community.

The team decided that it was important for Nate to live in the community, have a job that he enjoys, and maintain social relationships. Nate was described as a person who enjoys friends and needs help with daily living activities such as dressing, getting around the community, preparing meals, and shopping. The group also talked about Nate's need to be busy and his enjoyment of feeling productive. He was described as fun loving, liking music and sports, eager, wanting to learn, being good at art, loving, and liking people around. The group felt that Nate's remaining time in school should be spent preparing him for the next environment to which he would most likely move. Because he does not generalize easily, his day should be spent in community-based experiences.

Assessment Results

The results of the person-centered planning activity revealed that Nate needed to be prepared to go to work and live in the community. Because of his level of independent functioning, he would need ongoing support in all of his environments through supported employment, supported living situations, and special transportation. His learning style required that he be taught in the community in order to prepare him for life after school and that adult service agency involvement would be necessary.

Transition Planning

Nate's family discussed possible adult agencies that could provide services for Nate as he made the transition from school to adult living. They agreed that they needed to involve the local vocational rehabilitation counselor and a representative from the County Developmental Disabilities Service Center. Nate's school experience would need to include opportunities for supported employment, community-based experiences related to daily living skills, and speech and language, occupational therapy, and physical therapy services.

Statement of Needed Transition Services

The following statement of needed transition services was developed during Nate's IEP meeting:

Nate will continue working on alternate curriculum standards for the majority of the day and will enroll in electives at his high school. Nate and his parents will contact the Vocational Rehabilitation Office to begin the process of intake for services. Nate and his parents will also contact the County Developmental Disabilities Service Center to begin the process of intake for services. Nate and his parents will contact three supported living centers to determine the options available to Nate for independent living. Nate will continue to work with a job coach in the community in a variety of job settings for three hours each day to increase his vocational skills and to determine which job he is most interested in. Nate will also participate in daily living activities in the community such as shopping, laundry, and using public transportation at least 5 hours each week. Nate will continue to participate in the Circle of Friends group and Special Olympics.

Annual Goals and Objectives

Nate's parents and his teacher developed goals and objectives for two of the areas listed in the statement of needed transition services.

- *Annual Goal:* Nate will increase his vocational skills by increasing his production rate.
- *Short-Term Objective:* Nate will increase his production rate on a job related to light industry by 10% over baseline during a 2-week period.
- *Short-Term Objective:* Nate will increase his production rate on a job related to clerical tasks by 10% over baseline during a 2-week period.
- *Short-Term Objective:* Nate will increase his production rate on a job related to the service industry by 10% over baseline during a 2-week period.
- *Annual Goal:* Nate will demonstrate the ability to shop in a grocery store.
- *Short-Term Objective:* Given a picture grocery list with five items on it, Nate will find four out of five items within a 30-minute period in a grocery store near his home during three consecutive visits.
- *Short-Term Objective:* Nate will make a grocery list containing five items from food pictures and/or from coupons.
- *Short-Term Objective:* Nate will purchase a soft drink from a machine independently on 2 consecutive days.

Sample Transition Goals and Objectives

The following are suggested goals, objectives, and activities to assist the teacher in developing the student's transition plan. These goals, objectives, and activities are arranged by the roles adults are expected to assume as identified by Halpern (1994). The format of the goals and objectives varies across states and school districts. The goals and objectives included in the chapter are intended to serve as a springboard from which IEP teams develop individualized goals and objectives based on student need.

Although IDEA 2004 requires short-term objectives only for students receiving alternate assessments, we have included sample objectives for all goals, to be used as you feel appropriate.

Employment

- *Annual Goal 1:* The student will develop a realistic career plan.
  - ○ *Short-Term Objective:* The student will identify two career interests after completing [number] interest inventories.
  - ○ *Short-Term Objective:* The student will list four duties for each job by exploring [number] careers through job shadowing or work samples.
  - ○ *Short-Term Objective:* The student will select three (or more) possible careers and identify the training required for these careers.
  - ○ *Short-Term Objective:* The student will develop a list of possible occupations/jobs that are a match to personal interests.
- *Annual Goal 2:* The student will develop skills needed for employment in the occupation he or she has selected.
  - ○ *Short-Term Objective:* The student will demonstrate the occupationally specific skills needed for the occupation. These will be demonstrated on a community-based job and evaluated through a rating scale completed monthly by the employer.
  - ○ *Short-Term Objective:* The student will demonstrate competence in interviewing for a job by participating in a simulated interview and completing all of the steps on the interview rating form.
  - ○ *Short-Term Objective:* The student will list five job openings obtained from a variety of want ads in the newspaper.
  - ○ *Short-Term Objective:* The student will demonstrate competence in job skills such as attendance, task completion, work rate, and work quality as demonstrated by receiving a B or better on community-based work evaluations for a 9-week period.

Postsecondary Education

- *Annual Goal 1:* The student will enroll in a postsecondary education program that provides education in his or her area of career interest.
  - ○ *Short-Term Objective:* The student will identify [number] postsecondary education sites that offer programs related to his or her stated career interest.
  - ○ *Short-Term Objective:* The student will list the admittance procedures, prerequisites, and costs for each of the postsecondary sites identified.
  - ○ *Short-Term Objective:* The student will select the postsecondary education site that most closely corresponds with his or her occupational goals and resources and state the rationale for this choice.

o *Short-Term Objective:* After touring the postsecondary education sites, the student will identify his or her individual needs and required accommodations with admissions personnel.
o *Short-Term Objective:* The student will complete the application procedure for the postsecondary education site selected.
o *Short-Term Objective:* The student will correctly complete applications for financial aid for postsecondary education. Correctness will be defined as the provision of correct information in the correct blanks.

Maintaining a Home

- *Annual Goal 1:* The student will demonstrate the ability to secure appropriate housing.
  o *Short-Term Objective:* The student will report the amount of rent asked for in *[number]* ads for housing by *[date]*.
  o *Short-Term Objective:* After arranging for and completing a tour of *[number]* semi-independent residential options, the student will report back to the class five positive and five negative features of each one.
  o *Short-Term Objective:* Based on his or her interests and abilities, the student will select the most appropriate living site. The student will provide a rationale for this selection.

Involvement in the Community

- *Annual Goal 1:* The student will participate in leisure time and recreational activities.
  o *Short-Term Objective:* The student will identify *[number]* leisure/recreational activities or organizations in the community.
  o *Short-Term Objective:* The student will participate in *[number]* recreational activity (activities) each week for the next *[number]* weeks.
  o *Short-Term Objective:* The student will list *[number]* recreational activity (activities) sponsored by two community agencies during the next *[number]* months.
  o *Short-Term Objective:* The student will make plans with a peer to attend a spectator event.
  o *Short-Term Objective:* The student will attend an adult-supervised party and participate in age-appropriate activities.
- *Annual Goal 2:* The student will care for his or her own personal needs.
  o *Short-Term Objective:* The student will demonstrate the ability to sort laundry by light and dark with 100% accuracy by completing all of the steps on a checklist.

- o *Short-Term Objective:* The student will balance a checkbook ledger for a 1-month statement period with 100% accuracy.
- o *Short-Term Objective:* The student will demonstrate clean and sanitary dishwashing by completing all of the steps on a teacher checklist.
- o *Short-Term Objective:* The student will independently prepare *[number]* well-balanced meals using foods from the five basic food groups.
- o *Short-Term Objective:* From a set of pictures, the student will select the pictures that are of people who are dressed appropriately for work in an office environment with 100% accuracy.
- • *Annual Goal 3:* The student will obtain necessary financial/income assistance support.
  - o *Short-Term Objective:* The student will indicate whether he or she is eligible for income support from the Social Security Administration after contacting it to determine this eligibility.
  - o *Short-Term Objective:* The student will state whether he or she is eligible for vocational rehabilitation services.
  - o *Short-Term Objective:* The student will identify *[number]* agencies that provide financial assistance/income support.
  - o *Short-Term Objective:* The student will complete the application process for low income subsidized housing with 100% accuracy.
- • *Annual Goal 4:* The student will carry out civic responsibilities.
  - o *Short-Term Objective:* The student will register to vote by age 18.
  - o *Short-Term Objective:* The student will register for military service by age 18.
  - o *Short-Term Objective:* The student will use the public library to check out *[number]* books one time each month for the next *[number]* months.
  - o *Short-Term Objective:* The student will have his or her income tax forms completed by April 15th.
  - o *Short-Term Objective:* The student will provide volunteer service *[number]* time(s) per semester.
- • *Annual Goal 5:* The student will obtain appropriate medical service.
  - o *Short-Term Objective:* The student will list *[number]* situations that would lead him or her to seek assistance by dialing 911.
  - o *Short-Term Objective:* The student will name his or her hospital of preference.
  - o *Short-Term Objective:* The student will name his or her doctor and dentist.
  - o *Short-Term Objective:* The student will select an appropriate doctor and make an appointment in a nonemergency situation.
  - o *Short-Term Objective:* From a list of *[number]* physical conditions, the student will be able to identify which physical conditions require a doctor's care with 100% accuracy.
- • *Annual Goal 6:* The student will access community services to address personal needs in a variety of settings.

    o *Short-Term Objective:* The student will demonstrate the ability to make an appointment with the *[e.g., barber, hair stylist, dentist, doctor]* by calling the service provider and using his or her calendar to set the appointment.

    o *Short-Term Objective:* The student will identify his or her strengths and challenges to a person with whom he or she is familiar.

    o *Short-Term Objective:* The student will role-play describing his or her specific challenges/disability to a service provider such as a postsecondary counselor, group home administrator, or adult service agency employee. This role play will be evaluated through the use of a checklist containing the major steps for this process.

    o *Short-Term Objective:* The student will contact a community agency and ask for information about its services, following all of the steps generated in class discussion. The student's performance will be rated by the checklist of steps generated in class discussion.

- *Annual Goal 7:* The student will demonstrate the ability to seek effective insurance coverage.

    o *Short-Term Objective:* The student will list *[number]* types of insurance available to consumers.

    o *Short-Term Objective:* The student will list the types of insurance he or she wants to purchase and why.

    o *Short-Term Objective:* The student will identify the types of insurance carried by his or her family and whether or not he or she is covered by this insurance.

    o *Short-Term Objective:* The student will indicate what is needed to qualify for Medicaid.

    o *Short-Term Objective:* Through a role play, the student will demonstrate the steps involved in obtaining selected insurance coverage. Performance will be evaluated by a checklist containing the major steps in this process.

- *Annual Goal 8:* The student will use transportation within the community.

    o *Short-Term Objective:* The student will schedule his or her transportation through the special services system for *[number]* events.

    o *Short-Term Objective:* The student will obtain a driver's license.

    o *Short-Term Objective:* The student will use regular public transportation to get to work on time for 10 consecutive days.

Satisfactory Personal and Social Relationships

- *Annual Goal 1:* The student will demonstrate socially appropriate behaviors in a variety of settings.

    o *Short-Term Objective:* The student will role-play appropriate behaviors in given situations, with a rating by peers of 90% on the social behavior checklist.

    o *Short-Term Objective:* The student will appropriately greet and introduce himself or herself to a co-worker, completing all of the steps on a social skills checklist.

    o *Short-Term Objective:* The student will name/identify *[number]* types of relationships.

    o *Short-Term Objective:* The student will initiate a social activity with a peer.

    o *Short-Term Objective:* The student will identify the problem, when given a challenging situation, and list three possible solutions.

REFERENCES

Halpern, A. S. (1994). The transition of youth with disabilities to adult life: A position of the Division on Career Development and Transition. *Career Development for Exceptional Individuals, 17,* 115–124.

Individuals with Disabilities Education Improvement Act of 2004, 20 U.S.C. § 1400 (2004).

ADDITIONAL RESOURCES

Brolin, D. E., & Loyd, R. J. (2004). *Career development and transition services: A functional approach* (4th ed.). Upper Saddle River, NJ: Merrill-Prentice Hall.

Flexer, R. W., Simmons, T. J., Luft, P., & Baer, R. M. (2005). *Transition planning for secondary students with disabilities* (2nd ed.). Upper Saddle River, NJ: Merrill-Prentice Hall.

Kochhar-Bryant, C. A., & Bassett, D. S. (Eds.). (2002). *Aligning transition and standards-based education: Issues and strategies.* Arlington, VA: Council for Exceptional Children.

Sitlington, P. L., & Clark, G. M. (2006). *Transition education and services for students with disabilities* (4th ed.). Boston: Allyn & Bacon.

Trainor, A. A., Patton, J. R., & Clark, G. M. (2005). *Case studies in assessment for transition planning.* Austin, TX: Pro Ed.

5

Roles of Key Players

This chapter identifies the key players who can contribute to the transition assessment process for individuals with disabilities. The purpose of the chapter is to

- Identify who should participate in the transition assessment process.
- Present each player's role in the transition assessment process.
- Explain the types of information each stakeholder can provide.

The Individuals with Disabilities Education Improvement Act of 2004 (IDEA 2004) supports the notion that transition assessment and planning must involve a number of key stakeholders. The intent of the law is to ensure that transition assessment and planning procedures are conducted as a collaborative effort in which the various stakeholders have shared responsibility for planning, implementing, and evaluating districtwide transition policies and procedures. This language was included in part because special educators have historically assumed the majority of the responsibility for meeting students' educational planning needs, even though trained professionals from other fields and other interested persons could have provided important input and assistance.

Like comprehensive transition planning, assessing individuals with disabilities must become a shared responsibility. Assessing student needs, whether they are academic, vocational, or social, has often been the respon-sibility of a select few. School psychologists, guidance staff, special education teachers, vocational evaluators, and rehabilitation personnel have tradition-ally been relied upon to collect and interpret assessment data for the pur-poses of disability classification, special education program placement, and individual educational planning. The types of information gathered for these purposes are often insufficient with respect to the range and types of information needed to promote the student's transition from school to adulthood. Moreover, students with disabilities and their parents traditionally have not been invited to contribute to the assessment process or participate in joint decision making during the educational planning meetings. It is the intent of this chapter to specify the roles of each key stakeholder, including students with disabilities and their families.

WHO SHOULD PARTICIPATE AND WHAT INFORMATION CAN THEY PROVIDE?

Formal and informal transition assessment requires collection, examination, and interpretation of information from a variety of settings and from stakeholders relevant to the student's life. Transition assessment is often much more complex than traditional academic or achievement testing. Consequently, information from a wide variety of personnel is often required if the assessment is to be done successfully. The personnel who are discussed in this chapter include (a) students with disabilities; (b) family members; (c) special education teachers; (d) secondary and post-secondary educators; (e) school guidance personnel; (f) adult service providers; (g) employers, work experience staff, job coaches, and placement specialists; (h) support services personnel; (i) natural supports; (j) paraprofessionals; (k) middle school personnel; and (1) transition specialists. The types of information that each key player can contribute as part of the transition assessment process are also highlighted. See Table 5.1 for a list of the assessment roles for each key stakeholder.

Students With Disabilities

The most important player in the transition assessment process is the student. For too long, students with disabilities have been passive participants in educational planning and assessment activities. Students must become active players within all phases of individualized education program (IEP) planning, from learning how to participate during the IEP conference, to expressing preferences and interests, to assuming responsibility for implementing IEP goals and objectives. Thus, students with disabilities must also be at the center of all transition assessment activities.

Students must become knowledgeable about the purposes of assessment and the federal laws such as IDEA 2004 and the Americans with Disabilities Act (ADA) that guarantee their right of participation throughout each phase of assessment. Students also need to understand how assessment data may influence their access to transition services such as educational planning, placement into programs, instructional and curriculum

(Text continues on page 71)

Table 5.1   Roles of Key Players

Students With Disabilities	Family Members	Special Education Teachers	Secondary and Postsecondary Educators
• Express independent living needs/abilities • Express course-related interests • Express occupational and job-related interests • Express learning style preferences • Identify personal/social skills in need of improvement • Express leisure/recreation preferences • Identify community involvement interests • Express postsecondary education goals • Express postsecondary employment goals	• Foster independence by assigning specific responsibilities in the home • Explore community support, training, and employment options • Discuss future goals and adult realities with the student • Develop and support a work ethic common to the family culture • Discuss interests, abilities, and needs • Attend and participate in IEP meetings with the student • Support the student's efforts to direct his or her IEP and transition program • Complete parent and family surveys and needs assessments • Encourage the student's efforts to learn more about work demands and career options • Respond to follow-up surveys sent by local school systems	• Conduct interviews with family members and the student • Conduct situational assessments by observing student performance in a variety of school and community settings • Implement curriculum-based assessment activities • Administer formal assessments • Interpret assessment results gathered from other professionals • Interpret transition assessment data to students and transform it into functional goals and objectives on IEPs	• Provide course information to students one year before courses are taught • Provide information on course options • Provide information on eligibility and entry skill requirements • Provide information on the teaching style preferences of the instructor • Provide information on testing options • Provide information on evaluation and grading options • Provide information on performance standards and learner outcomes associated with a particular course • Observe and record student performance in class in regard to attendance and safety • Observe and record student performance in cooperative group behavior

(Continued)

Table 5.1 (Continued)

Students with Disabilities	Family Members	Special Education Teachers	Secondary and Postsecondary Educators
	• Jointly plan for financial, living, health, leisure, and transportation needs		• Observe and record student performance on tests, quizzes, and project completion • Observe and record student performance on general progress toward exit-level skills and learner outcomes
School Guidance Personnel	*Adult Service Providers*	*Employers, Work Experience Staff, Job Coaches, and Placement Specialists*	*Support Services Personnel*
• Administer formal and informal interest surveys as early as possible • Provide post-assessment counseling • Assist in helping students express their individual strengths, limitations, and preferences • Assist students in enrolling in secondary school courses consistent with their interests, needs, and learning preferences • Provide information for future planning in postsecondary education, employment, military, and/or community options	• Participate in transition assessment activities when the student is at least 16 years of age • Communicate information about their agencies' services to individuals with disabilities • Provide a linkage to the school agencies by collaborating with IEP and assessment teams • Attend IEP meetings with the student and family	• Provide information on entry-level job skills • Provide information on possible workplace accommodation options • Provide information on supported employment options • Provide information on possible apprenticeship options • Provide information on technology skills requirements • Observe and record student's workplace readiness • Observe and record student's ability to follow directions and cooperate with coworkers	• Participate in the transition assessment process • Provide information on the student's special needs: psychological testing, physical and rehabilitation therapies, and community support services

School Guidance Personnel	Adult Service Providers	Employers, Work Experience Staff, Job Coaches, and Placement Specialists	Support Services Personnel
• Participate in the IEP process		• Observe and record the student's work ethic, behavior, and productivity level • Observe and record the student's ability to work under supervision and accept criticism • Observe and record the student's job-related interest and motivation	
Natural Supports	**Paraprofessionals**	**Middle School Personnel**	**Transition Specialists**
• Discuss leisure and recreation issues and concerns • Discuss changes in occupational interests • Provide ongoing or modified assistive technology • Help solve educational and/or workplace problems • Discuss social skill needs and abilities • Assist with job development needs and skills • Help with job training needs and skills	• Score and record assessment results • Provide instructional support in general education classes • Develop instructional accommodations • Develop curricular accommodations • Chart behavior observations • Monitor and record progress toward IEP goals • Communicate with parents regarding student goal attainment	• Assess the occupational interests of students • Assess the vocational ability of students • Assess the preferred learning styles of students • Maintain a portfolio documenting assessment results • Assess the entry level skills of high school courses • Ensure students acquire entry level skills prior to high school entry	• Review/secure vocational ability instruments for use within the district • Review/secure occupational interest instruments for use within the district • Review/secure learning style instruments for use within the district • Review/secure self-determination assessment tools for use within the district • Conduct assessments for students with disabilities

(Continued)

Table 5.1 (Continued)

Natural Supports	Paraprofessionals	Middle School Personnel	Transition Specialists
• Work on interaction skills with teachers and employers	• Document student performance in general education settings	• Ensure that needed supports are indicated on IEPs • Provide guidance and counseling for high school course enrollment • Ensure that students actively participate in IEP meetings	• Record assessment results in student portfolios • Interpret assessment results for assessment IEP team • Facilitate student enrollment in courses that are consistent with interests and abilities • Contact adult support agencies for supplementary assessments and supports • Assist the student with applications to postsecondary educational programs • Assist the student with applications for postsecondary employment

modifications, work experience, and their preparation for the transition into living, working, and postsecondary education environments. It must also be clear to students that transition assessment is a process that will promote their ability to become self-advocates. Students who are aware of their abilities, preferences, future goals, and instructional needs will be well positioned to express them prior to and during educational planning meetings and with individual teachers and adult service providers after program placement has occurred.

Students with disabilities must provide the context for transition assessment and all related data-gathering activities. They can provide this context by expressing their future goals and aspirations concerning the five adult role domains of employment, postsecondary education, independent living, community involvement, and personal/social relationships. After the student has expressed postsecondary goals and aspirations, transition assessment activities must be oriented toward the environments in which the student will function. For example, a student who expresses an interest in attending business courses at a local community college after high school graduation has provided an important context for further assessment activities. First, the student, teacher, and family members must review grades, performance in any business-related work experiences, and performance in any high school business courses. Then, information regarding the community college business courses, enrollment procedures and requirements, academic support services, living accommodations, and financial support must be collected.

For a student with severe disabilities, the family, student, and teacher may decide to investigate recreation opportunities in the community. First, the student and family should be asked to identify activities of interest. Then, the teacher can explore support options available to the student in the community. Once these have been determined, the student should be allowed to try out the recreation activities while receiving the support needed.

The extent of student participation in transition assessment activities depends upon the student and the type of assessment questions being asked. In general, students with disabilities should participate in transition assessment in the following ways:

- Expressing independent living needs/abilities
- Expressing course-related interests
- Expressing occupational and job-related interests
- Expressing learning style preferences
- Identifying personal-social skills in need of improvement
- Expressing leisure/recreation preferences
- Identifying community involvement interests
- Expressing postsecondary education goals
- Expressing postsecondary employment goals

Family Members

Although the student is the most essential player in the transition assessment process, family members should also play an important role in transition assessment and planning activities. Members of the family who can contribute valuable information include parents, brothers and sisters, extended family members (such as aunts and uncles and grandparents), and others regarded as family, such as foster parents, guardians, and close family friends. Family members can offer a unique perspective on a student with disabilities. They often have the most insight regarding the student's history and personal strengths and limitations, as well as an understanding of the student's self-esteem and other interpersonal concerns. This can be especially true for students from multicultural and/or minority backgrounds. Due to the cultural bias of many formal assessment approaches, it is critical that family members be asked to provide information about the student and the culture that cannot be obtained reliably from other sources. Families may also have specific educational goals in mind that are based on cultural beliefs and customs. For students with moderate and severe disabilities, family members are often the foundation of transition planning, and they must be actively involved in the assessment process.

To become active participants in assessment activities, educational planning, and implementation of IEP transition goals, family members must become knowledgeable about specific issues that may impact the family member with disabilities. An awareness of federal and state legislation, for example, will enable the family to advocate for instructional and/or support services that are tied directly to the assessed needs of the student. In addition, family members who understand the full range of school and postsecondary program options can work with the student and other educational planners to advocate for participation in courses and community experiences that best prepare him or her for further education and/or employment in the field of interest.

Clearly, a family that is informed about legal issues, secondary and postsecondary program options, support services, community living, and employment opportunities will be positioned to contribute much to the transition assessment process. Family members can participate further in this process by implementing, observing, and recording the following activities:

- Fostering independence by assigning specific responsibilities in the home
- Exploring community support, education, and employment options
- Discussing future goals and adult realities with the student
- Developing and supporting a work ethic common to the family culture
- Discussing interests, abilities, and needs
- Attending and participating in IEP meetings with the student

- Supporting the student's efforts to direct his or her IEP and transition planning
- Completing parent and family surveys and needs assessments
- Encouraging the student's efforts to learn more about work demands and career options
- Responding to follow-up surveys sent by the local school system
- Jointly planning for financial, living, health, leisure, and transportation needs

Family members are in a unique position to assist students in developing a positive attitude about their future. Issues regarding future living arrangements, postsecondary education, employment, community involvement, and personal/social options should be openly discussed among the family members early in the high school years. Because the family may have the greatest influence on the student's perception of self, it is vital that they be supportive of his or her future goals and aspirations. It is equally important that family members encourage and support student decision making and student self-determination so the student can realize his or her goals and aspirations as independently as possible.

Special Education Teachers

The diverse roles that special education teachers can play throughout the transition assessment process can range from gathering assessment data to planning effective instruction and services. An important role many special education teachers assume with respect to transition assessment is that of service coordinator. As service coordinators, special education teachers facilitate the development of student portfolios or other documents providing a broad picture of student performance and skills that can be beneficial to comprehensive transition planning. To conduct transition planning, information from a wide variety of sources must be collected and reviewed. Although there are numerous stakeholders in this process, special education staff, in the role of service coordinators, are often asked to facilitate and organize this effort.

In this role special education staff need to understand what information should be collected, where the information is located, and whom to contact to gather the data. For example, special educators should identify the range of pertinent information that is available from personnel within the school and that which is available from family members and community sources. Special education personnel must also collaborate with the various stakeholders to ensure that they understand the transition assessment process and how data they provide can assist in the delivery of transition services.

Special education teachers need to be able to conduct certain types of assessment activities to complement data collected from other sources.

A sample of transition assessment activities that are appropriate for special educators include the following:

- Conducting interviews with family members and the student
- Conducting situational assessments by observing student performance in a variety of school and community settings
- Implementing curriculum-based assessment activities
- Administering formal assessments
- Interpreting assessment results gathered from other professionals
- Interpreting transition assessment data to students and transforming it into functional goals and objectives on IEPs

Another important role that special educators can play in the assessment process is preparing students to participate in assessment activities and helping them understand the results of various assessments. Students must be made fully aware of the reasons for assessment activities, the people who will be involved in the process, and how assessment data can assist in educational planning for their future. Issues related to self-determination need to be addressed throughout the assessment process and in advance of any and all IEP meetings. This will ensure that many students are prepared to express their needs, strengths, preferences, interests, and long-term goals in conjunction with planning activities. For students with more severe disabilities, special educators must assist parents and students in understanding assessment results and planning activities that contribute to identifying vocational and community living options.

Collaborating with families is yet another important role of special education instructors. Special education teachers can provide family members with information that enables them to become active participants in the transition assessment process. Information that special education teachers can share with family members includes (a) legal rights and responsibilities, (b) school support services, (c) work experience opportunities, (d) adult support services, and (e) postsecondary education and employment options. Family members who are made aware of the full continuum of available programs and support service options will be more likely to support decisions that are based on the needs and realistic aspirations of the student.

Secondary and Postsecondary Educators

Secondary and postsecondary general and career and technical educators can assist in creating meaningful linkages between school and work by providing information about the courses they teach to special educators, students, and family members at least one year before the student qualifies to enroll in such courses. Course-related information that can be gathered as part of transition assessment procedures includes (a) course options, (b) eligibility and entry-level skill requirements, (c) teaching style preferences of the instructor, (d) testing options, (e) evaluation and grading options, and (f) performance standards and learner outcomes associated with particular courses. Information of this type will be of maximum use if it is collected and shared well in advance of any placement decisions. This will allow students the time to advocate for enrollment in courses that are consistent with their interests, preferences, and abilities.

Increasing access to general and career and technical education at the secondary and postsecondary level is an important goal of transition assessment activities. Once students are enrolled in appropriate courses, however, it will be necessary to gather information about their performance within the general and career and technical education setting. General and career and technical educators can observe and document student performance related to attendance, safety, cooperative group behavior, test and quiz scores, project completion, and general progress toward exit-level skills and learner outcomes. In addition to monitoring student performance within the classroom or lab, general and career and technical educators must communicate their observations to special education personnel or support staff who are responsible for coordinating instructional support services for students. General and career and technical educators, special educators, and support staff can then work in collaboration with the student to determine whether modifications to the curriculum or adaptations to instructional services are needed.

Curriculum information will enable the transition assessment planners to identify which skills a student needs in order to enter a particular program, which entry-level skills are or are not currently possessed by the student, and which skills should be prioritized on the IEP for immediate instruction by special educators and/or regular educators.

It is important to collect curriculum and instructional information as part of the transition assessment process. These types of data can be most efficiently gathered by face-to-face interactions between special education staff and general and career and technical educators. A procedure that can be used to record information of this type is called a program inventory. A sample program inventory form for a career and technical education program is provided in Appendix E.

School Guidance Personnel

School guidance and counseling personnel have a long history of providing routine assessment services for students leaving the school system and entering postsecondary training and/or employment settings. However, the extent of assessment services that counselors have provided for individuals with disabilities has varied greatly from district to district. This may be due, in part, to a fundamental lack of understanding about the assessment needs of individuals with disabilities and the role that guidance personnel can play in accommodating these needs.

School guidance personnel can assist in the transition assessment process by assessing the occupational interests and vocational abilities of students at various times. Some students should have their interests identified while in middle school and before decisions are made regarding high school course placement. School guidance staff can administer formal and informal interest surveys to students with disabilities at this juncture and then provide post-assessment counseling so students can learn to understand and express their individual strengths, limitations, and preferences. Guidance staff should also assist students in enrolling in high school courses that are consistent with their needs, strengths, preferences, and interests. For students with more severe disabilities, guidance personnel can participate in interviews with the student, parents, and other family members to determine the student's interests, needs, and community support options.

To help prepare students for adult life, guidance personnel can once again examine occupational interests, abilities, and preferences. While discussing the assessment results with individual students, guidance staff can promote planning for the future by providing information about postsecondary educational, employment, military, and/or other community options that are consistent with transition assessment data. Guidance staff can also refer students to other evaluators and/or adult service providers, such as vocational rehabilitation agencies, if additional assessment information is needed. Like other stakeholders in transition assessment, guidance personnel need to be active participants in all phases of the IEP process. This will ensure that the information collected by guidance staff is communicated to all of the IEP participants and that the data are taken into consideration during the educational planning process.

Adult Service Providers

Adult service providers such as Vocational Rehabilitation, Workforce Development, and postsecondary institutions play an integral role in the school-to-postsecondary-setting transition process. Before a student can make realistic decisions about education or employment pursuits after high school, the continuum of adult service options must be fully explored. The number and types of adult support service options are often determined by the general location of the school. Typically, schools that are located near an urban community have access to a greater number of adult support services than school districts in rural areas. Nevertheless, it is necessary for both urban and rural schools to establish meaningful interagency linkages as a result of comprehensive assessment activities.

Although the number of adult support options may be influenced by location, there are many important contributions adult service providers can make that will assist students with disabilities in making successful school-to-adult-life transitions in either urban or rural communities. First, adult service providers should be invited to be members of the transition assessment and the IEP teams. As team members, adult service providers will have a forum to share information about their agencies with other stakeholders. Students, family members, special education staff, and other members of the transition assessment or IEP teams can be given information about agency services such as assessment/evaluation services, eligibility requirements, job coaching and job placement assistance, financial supports, and independent living options. It is critical that team members understand the continuum of adult support options available to students with disabilities in the local community. Once this information has been shared, transition assessment planners can coordinate meaningful linkages between individual students and appropriate adult service agencies.

Employers, Work Experience Staff, Job Coaches, and Placement Specialists

Although some students with disabilities will make the transition from secondary schools to postsecondary educational settings and then to employment, others will move into competitive or supported employment positions immediately after high school. Ideally, these students will enter the job market with the entry-level skills they need to be employed successfully. Unfortunately, numerous studies have shown that students with disabilities often leave the public schools underprepared for immediate entry into the labor force. The transition assessment process should provide a forum for employers to communicate information about their businesses or industries to school personnel. This will enable transition assessment planners to develop and implement educational plans that target the entry-level job skills and work behaviors required by local employers.

As assessment team members, employers can contribute job-related information that will help facilitate the development of IEP/transition plans. Employers can identify what skills the student needs to acquire in order to obtain a particular job. They can also make recommendations as to how the school can assist the student in learning the entry-level job skills. In addition, employers and school personnel such as work experience coordinators, job coaches, and job placement staff are in a unique position to observe and assess students in community work settings. Students who are participating in work experience programs, vocational cooperative education programs, or apprenticeships can have their work behavior assessed by employers and school staff through direct observation at the job site.

To facilitate effective school-to-work transition planning, assessment personnel must seek out employers to provide essential job-related information. The types of information employers can provide may include the following:

- Entry-level job skills
- Workplace accommodation options
- Supported employment options

- Apprenticeship options
- Technology skills requirements
- Environmental work conditions

Employers, work experience staff, job coaches, and job placement specialists can also provide information to educational planners about students' on-the-job performance. Worker-related information that can be recorded by employers and other work staff may include the following:

- Workplace readiness skills
- Ability to follow directions
- Coworker relationships
- Productivity levels
- Job-related interests
- Work ethics and behavior
- Acceptance of criticism/supervision

Support Services Personnel

Support services personnel such as school psychologists, occupational therapists, physical therapists, consultants, speech and hearing therapists, and social workers are also stakeholders in the transition assessment process. Support personnel often provide a wide range of supports to students with disabilities. Psychological testing results, physical and occupational therapy screening data, and other social or family information must become part of the transition assessment database. Information that is collected as a result of support staff assessment and screening should be shared with IEP and transition assessment team members. This will ensure that appropriate support services are indicated on IEPs and that services are provided as needed.

Support services staff can also provide information that will impact the overall school-to-adult-life transition planning process for students with disabilities. In many cases, students receiving support services in the secondary school setting will need continued support services in postsecondary settings. A student, for example, who is receiving taped textbook services in high school due to a visual disability or a significant reading deficit will need to receive compatible accommodations in postsecondary educational and/or work settings. In cases such as these, support services staff can assist in matching student needs to specific supports or workplace accommodations that will be required in future settings.

Natural Supports

While the stakeholders mentioned in this chapter can play important roles with respect to the transition assessment process, other people such as student peers, coworkers, and friends can also provide helpful information to the individual with disabilities and to the transition assessment team.

These persons are regarded as "natural supports" because they live, attend school, and work in the same settings as the individuals with disabilities. Consequently, they can often provide support within the context of natural environments at school, at work, and in the community.

Student peers, friends, and coworkers can be asked to make observations about persons with disabilities within these natural environments. Observational information that should be collected and shared with transition assessment personnel may include the following:

- Leisure and recreation issues and concerns
- Changes in occupational interests
- Need for ongoing or modified assistive technology
- Ability to solve educational and/or workplace problems
- Social skill needs and abilities
- Job development needs and skills
- Job training needs and skills
- Interaction skills with teachers and employers

Paraprofessionals

Due to the educational, medical, and social needs experienced by students with disabilities, many special education programs are supported by paraprofessionals who assist the special or general education teacher within the context of the classroom setting. These paraprofessionals, sometimes known as program assistants or aides, provide an invaluable service to the teacher and to students with disabilities. Many special education programs include students with a wide range of instructional, medical, and behavioral needs that are quite difficult for a single teacher to address alone. Consequently, paraprofessionals often are asked to assume very important roles to ensure that each student is provided with quality instruction and essential curricular accommodations. Important functions that paraprofessionals can provide related to transition planning include the following:

- Scoring and recording assessment results
- Providing instructional support in general education classes
- Developing instructional accommodations
- Developing curricular accommodations
- Charting behavioral observations
- Monitoring and recording progress toward IEP goals
- Communicating with parents regarding student goal attainment
- Documenting student performance in general education settings

Middle School Personnel

Although many transition assessment activities take place while the student with disabilities is enrolled in high school, middle school personnel play a critical role in preparing the student to make the transition from middle school to high school. To ensure that students with disabilities are placed in secondary programs that are consistent with expressed interests and abilities, middle school teachers and support personnel can do the following:

- Assess the occupational interests of students
- Assess the vocational ability of students
- Assess the preferred learning styles of students
- Maintain a portfolio documenting assessment results
- Assess the entry-level skills of high school courses
- Ensure that students acquire entry-level skills prior to high school entry
- Ensure that needed supports are indicated on IEPs
- Provide guidance and counseling for high school course enrollment
- Ensure that students actively participate in IEP meetings

Transition Specialists

The final stakeholder to be discussed in this chapter is the transition specialist. As a result of funding from the United States Office of Special Education and Rehabilitation Services (OSERS) throughout the late eighties and early nineties, numerous universities throughout the country were awarded federal grants to develop graduate level training programs. The intent of these programs was to offer coursework leading to a master's degree or alternative transition specialist certificate. Graduates of these programs (often known as transition specialists) acquired knowledge and skills associated with the development, implementation, and supervision of districtwide transition planning. Typically, a transition specialist is a special education teacher who spends part of the day in the classroom providing instruction to students with disabilities and the remainder of the day designing, organizing ,and implementing transition assessment and planning activities. Although the complete list of activities that revolve around a transition specialist is not appropriate for this chapter, transition specialist activities related to transition assessment may include the following:

- Reviewing/securing vocational ability instruments for use within the district
- Reviewing/securing occupational interest instruments for use within the district
- Reviewing/securing learning style instruments for use within the district
- Reviewing/securing self-determination assessment tools for use within the district
- Conducting assessments for students with disabilities
- Recording assessment results on student portfolios

- Interpreting assessment results for assessment IEP team
- Facilitating student enrollment in courses that are consistent with interests and abilities
- Contacting adult support agencies for supplementary assessments and supports
- Assisting the student with applications to postsecondary educational programs
- Assisting the student with applications for postsecondary employment

SUMMARY

This chapter identified the key players in the transition assessment process and outlined the types of information that each key player could contribute and the various ways in which the information could be used to promote effective transition planning for students with disabilities. A fundamental outcome of transition assessment activities is to ensure that students with disabilities are able to participate as fully as possible in secondary, postsecondary, and adult settings of their choice. These outcomes will be realized by more students with disabilities if each and every stakeholder fully participates as a team member in transition assessment and planning activities.

REFERENCES

Americans with Disabilities Act of 1990, 42 U.S.C. § 12101(1990).
Individuals with Disabilities Education Improvement Act of 2004, 20 U.S.C. § 1400 (2004).

ADDITIONAL RESOURCES

DeFur, S. H., & Patton, J. R. (1999). *Transition and school-based services: Interdisciplinary perspectives for enhancing the transition process.* Austin, TX: Pro-Ed.
Gavin, M. K., Gugerty, J. J., Hazelkorn, M. N., Kellogg, A., Lombard, R. C., & Warden, R. (1993). *Designated vocational instruction: A resource and planning guide.* Madison: Wisconsin Department of Public Instruction.
Miller, R. J., Lombard, R. C., & Corbey, S. A. (2007). *Transition assessment: Planning transition and IEP development for youth with mild to moderate disabilities.* Boston: Allyn & Bacon.
Nisbet, J. (1992). *Natural supports in school, at work, and in the community for people with severe disabilities.* Baltimore: Paul H. Brookes.

6

Methods of Gathering Information

T his chapter provides an overview of methods that practitioners can use to collect assessment data throughout the transition planning process. The goals are

- To describe methods of assessing individuals
- To describe methods of assessing current and future living, working, and educational environments

There is a wealth of information in the general education, special education, rehabilitation, and career and technical education literature on methods and models of assessment that identify the community, independent living, vocational, instructional, and personal/social strengths and needs of individuals with disabilities. It is necessary to determine what methods of assessment are needed at various transition points for individuals with disabilities to make appropriate placement and planning decisions. However, this does not mean that new methods and models of assessment are needed to facilitate transition planning.

Transition assessment does require professionals to think beyond commonly used assessment practices such as standardized tests and to move toward conducting assessments in actual life contexts such as community-based living situations, job sites, and postsecondary education settings. This move toward more authentic assessment can also be achieved in educational settings by using performance samples. The transition assessment process should focus on deciding what type of assessment data to collect, when to collect it, who will collect the data, and how the results will be used. Assessment data must come from many sources and be updated periodically to ensure that students' transition goals are appropriate and realistic. Most important, the results of the assessment process must be used to develop realistic transition goals during the Individualized Education Program (IEP) planning process and the development of the course of study. In addition, the results of the transition assessment process must be incorporated into the Summary of Performance (SOP), as the student is transitioning to adult life.

Transition assessment is an ongoing process that takes place during the middle and high school years. This process may need to be continued throughout the adult years for some individuals with disabilities to determine the support and accommodations they will need to be as independent as possible in their adult lives. Data should be collected that will lead to appropriate postsecondary goals in the areas of independent living and community involvement, employment, postsecondary education, and personal and social relationships. Sitlington, Neubert, and Leconte (1997, p. 75) suggested the following guidelines for selecting methods used in the transition assessment process:

- Assessment methods must be tailored to the types of information needed and the decisions to be made regarding transition planning and various postsecondary outcomes
- Specific methods selected must be appropriate for the learning characteristics of the individual, including cultural and linguistic differences
- Assessment methods must incorporate assistive technology or accommodations that will allow an individual to demonstrate his or her abilities and potential
- Assessment methods must occur in environments that resemble actual vocational training, employment, independent living, or community environments
- Assessment methods must produce outcomes that contribute to ongoing development, planning, and implementation of "next steps" in the individual's transition process
- Assessment methods must be varied and include a sequence of activities that sample an individual's behavior and skills over time
- Assessment data must be verified by more than one method and by more than one person
- Assessment data must be synthesized and interpreted to individuals with disabilities, their families, and transition team members
- Assessment data and the results of the assessment process must be documented in a format that can be used to facilitate transition planning

This chapter provides an overview of methods that can be used in transition assessment for gathering information about individuals and on their current or future living, working, and educational environments. Each method is briefly described along with a discussion of the types of information that can be collected using that method. Chapter 7 provides a framework for using this information to match an individual with appropriate environments, for identifying accommodations and supports the individual will need in a specific environment, and for developing the SOP required by the Individuals with Disabilities Education Improvement Act of 2004 (IDEA 2004), as the individual is transitioning into adult life.

METHODS OF GATHERING INFORMATION ABOUT INDIVIDUALS

This section presents an overview of basic methods of gathering information about the individual that can be used as you assist the student in planning for the transition from school to all aspects of adult life. It begins with the methods that are most removed from actual adult environments in which the individual will build his or her life, and ends with situational assessment, which focuses on collecting information as individuals live, work, and study in environments as close as possible to those in which they will participate as adults. The methods covered are (a) analysis of background information, (b) interviews, (c) standardized tests, (d) curriculum-based assessment techniques, (e) performance samples, (f) behavioral observation techniques, and (g) situational assessment.

Analysis of Background Information

One of the first sources of information about the student should be previous records, which contain observations of previous teachers, support staff, and staff from other agencies (e.g., Mental Health or Vocational Rehabilitation) who have worked with the individual. In addition to the cumulative folder, there are often other records kept by teachers or support staff who have worked with the student. Often these other records contain more useful information than the "official" student files. Be sure that you also review past Individualized Education Programs (IEPs) with particular emphasis on transition-related objectives and activities contained in them. Also ask for any additional formal and informal assessments that have been conducted with the student. Although all of this information should be in the student's official files, this often is not the case. If other youth and adult service agencies have been working with the individual, ask whether you can review their information, after receiving appropriate releases of information from the family or the individual.

Student portfolios provide valuable information that has been selected by the student and staff as representative of the student's interests, goals, and finest work. In fact, a transition portfolio is an excellent means of organizing and summarizing all of the transition assessment and transition-planning activities in which the student has participated (Neubert & Moon, 2000). These and other existing records often contain a wealth of information about the strengths and interests of the individual, as well as the areas on which the individual needs to focus. This information may be in the form of formal and informal assessment results; comments of previous teachers, guidance counselors, and other support staff and adult service providers; and records of IEP meetings. The records may also contain information about the experiences the individual has had in high school and in the community related to living and employment, and the techniques and approaches that have worked (or not worked) with the individual in the past. In addition, they may contain information about health-related issues. If transition planning activities have been conducted with the student in previous years, it is enlightening to review the trends in the student's expressed interests and preferences during these years.

It is important to remember in reviewing records, however, that individuals may react differently to new teachers and to new classroom environments or new living or work environments. They may enter these environments with a changed attitude. Thus, while you should consider previous information, take time to form opinions based on your own observations and experiences with the student, as well as his or her self-reports.

Interviews

Interviews with the student, family members, former teachers, friends, counselors, other support staff, and former employers may be one of the best sources of information about how the individual functions in the real world and what he or she would like to do as an adult. Interviews of people who know students well can uncover rich information. Frequently, brothers and sisters of students have more realistic and accurate information than their parents about their siblings' long-term goals, social and personal aspirations, and abilities. Siblings are major stakeholders in the students' transition, since they may one day assume responsibility for their brothers and sisters who have disabilities.

Steps in Conducting Interviews

Interviews may follow a structured format or develop as the interview is proceeding. To make the best use of the interview process and obtain consistent information across interviews, however, you should follow the steps listed on the next page.

- Come prepared with a set of specific questions.
- Be flexible in following up on a specific question and obtaining clarifying or additional information. Always return, however, to your basic list of questions.
- Conduct the interview in person, if possible, so that you can pick up on subtle cues from the person being interviewed, such as facial expressions and shifts in body posture.
- Make the purpose of the interview clear and assure the interviewee that *there are no right or wrong answers.*
- Make the person as comfortable as possible. It may be a good idea to provide the person with a copy of the questions before the actual interview, especially if some of the questions require recall of specific facts or events from the past.
- Write down enough information during the interview so you can remember the individual's responses. *Take time right after the interview to complete your notes.*
- Try not to lead the person or insert your own personal biases or responses into the questions. Allow the person enough time to organize the answer before speaking. Also allow the person to respond as thoroughly as he or she chooses to a specific question.

The interview process is one of the most useful in gathering relevant information about how the student has functioned in real-life situations and in determining the goals the student and family have related to adult life. It does not require reading or writing on the part of the person being interviewed. It also allows you to clarify any responses that you do not understand, pursue answers to incomplete responses, and verify or validate information collected through other methods.

A wide range of information can be gathered through the interview process. The strength of this process is that it provides information about what is actually happening *now* in the individual's life, what has happened in the *past,* and what the interviewee would like to see happen in the *future.* This information can include such areas as the responsibilities the individual assumes at home related to daily living skills, friendships, activities the individual enjoys, odd jobs the student has held, and academic subjects in which the student excels. The interview process can also uncover the goals that the individual has in the areas of living, working, and postsecondary education, and how these goals relate to those held by the individual's family.

While interviews may provide a great deal of information, there are some drawbacks to this technique. First, it can be time consuming, both in terms of arranging the interviews and actually collecting the information. Second, if you do not enter the interview with a specific set of questions and keep the interview focused on these questions, you may not gather the information you set out to gather. Finally, the person being interviewed may feel intimidated and may provide responses he or she feels you want to hear.

Person-Centered Planning

Although person-centered planning is not always viewed as an assessment process, we see it as a valuable assessment tool closely related to the interview process described in the preceding paragraphs. Individual choice is a primary policy theme reflected across all of the legislation discussed in Chapter 1. To guide the planning process effectively, students must be aware of their needs and their strengths, preferences, and interests, and how these relate to community-based living, work, postsecondary education, and personal and social relationships. The person-centered planning approach can play a major role in incorporating student choice into the transition assessment process.

Person-centered planning and personal futures planning were created with the expectation that they would be implemented according to the philosophy and values on which they were based—that no one has a right to plan for another person's life without that individual's participation, permission, or request (Sax, 2002). The commitment must be to a long-term process, rather than a single meeting, and facilitators and participants must be willing to listen to the focus individual and be prepared to hear statements that may not always be what they want to hear.

As Clark (2007) stated, person-centered planning brings together the focus person with a variety of stakeholders in that person's current and future life, and helps loosen the constraints of school and service agency approaches to working with students with disabilities. The process results in a plan of action that is based on preferences and strengths of the individual and is developed so specifically that IEP goals, objectives, and action statements also serve as documentation for the IDEA 2004 requirement that the student be a part of the transition planning process.

Schwartz, Holburn, and Jacobson (2000, p. 238) identified eight key features of person-centered planning, regardless of the approach:

1. The person's activities, services, and supports are based on his or her dreams, interests, preferences, strengths, and capacities.

2. The person and people important to him or her are included in lifestyle planning and have the opportunity to exercise control and make informed decisions.

3. The person has meaningful choices, with decisions based on his or her experiences.

4. The person uses, when possible, natural and community supports.

5. Activities, supports, and services foster skills to achieve personal relationships, community inclusion, dignity, and respect.

6. The person's opportunities and experiences are maximized and flexibility is enhanced within existing regulatory and funding constraints.

7. Planning is collaborative and recurring and involves an ongoing commitment to the person.

8. The person is satisfied with his or her relationships, home, and daily routine.

This approach also strengthens the capacity of the individuals and their families together to build formal and informal support circles that ensure that the young adult will be active in family and community life.

Standardized Tests

Standardized tests are farther removed from tasks required in the real world of employment and adult community living than most of the other techniques presented in this chapter, but they do relate to current academic goals and demands and may relate to skills needed in postsecondary education and training programs. These instruments are usually available from commercial publishers. Examples include tests of academic achievement, vocational interest, functional living skills, self-concept, and learning styles.

These instruments generally fall into two categories: norm referenced and objective referenced. In many cases, objectives take the form of competencies. Salvia and Ysseldyke (2004, p. 691) provided the following definitions for these terms:

- *Norm-referenced devices.* Tests that compare an individual's performance to the performance of his or her peers.
- *Objective-referenced assessment.* Tests referenced to specific instructional objectives rather than to the performance of a peer group or norm group.

Although some of these tests must be administered by individuals formally trained in test administration and interpretation, there are a number of tests that can be administered by the classroom teacher or residential supervisor. Other sources (Clark, 2007; Whitfield, Feller, & Wood, 2007) have summarized the major standardized tests related to the major areas of transition. A chart characterizing the major tests available is included as Appendix B.

If you choose to use standardized tests as one method of gathering information about the student, there are some questions you should ask yourself:

- Will the content and format of the results be helpful to you, the student, and others working with the student?
- Does the test manual provide information about its reliability (how consistent it is) and its validity (whether it measures what it says it measures)? Is the test reliable and valid?
- If the test is one that compares the results to the performance of others (a norming group), is the norming group one to whom you want to compare your students?

- Will the student be able to read the questions? If not can they be read to him or her?
- Even if the questions are read aloud, will the student understand the questions, and do the responses have a reasonable chance of reflecting the student's knowledge or feelings?
- Does the student have enough experience to relate to the situations presented in the test?

When many people think of assessment, they think mainly of these formal instruments. One advantage of this approach is that it provides an "official-looking" score and a standardized method of gathering specific information. Like any of the other techniques described in this chapter, standardized tests should not be used as the only method of gathering the information you need to assist the student and family in transition planning. Many professionals use these instruments as a starting point to plan other assessment activities or to engage in discussion with the student.

Standardized tests can also provide information about the knowledge level of the student related to functional living areas (e.g., managing money, maintaining a home, shopping) and to specific occupations or occupational clusters. However, they do not provide information about how well the individual applies this knowledge in real-life situations. In addition, the ability of the student to perform well on these instruments depends not only on knowledge, but also on the amount of experience the student has had with the situations presented in the test.

Curriculum-Based Assessment Techniques

One of the major thrusts in the field of education is curriculum-based assessment (CBA). This is assessment that is based on what is contained in the curriculum. Curriculum-based assessment is really an *approach* rather than one specific method. This approach is included here, however, because it is often viewed as a specific assessment technique and is being used increasingly in content-area classes such as math and English, as well as in career and technical education programs. Curriculum-based assessment instruments can be developed by teachers or other staff and focus on the content being taught. Specific curriculum-based assessment techniques include criterion-referenced testing, domain-referenced testing, curriculum-based measurement, and portfolio assessment. Each of these approaches is discussed in the following paragraphs. They can be used to gather information related to planning for current and future living, working, or educational environments.

Criterion-Referenced Testing

The criterion-referenced testing approach compares the individual's performance to a pre-established level of performance (e.g., 80%), rather than to the performance of others or to a set of norms. In this approach the emphasis is on the knowledge or skills needed for a specific content area and whether the individual has demonstrated mastery of this knowledge. Results of the assessment would indicate, for example, that a student scored 70% on two-digit by one-digit multiplication problems and 40% on two-digit by two-digit multiplication. The criterion-referenced testing approach is used primarily in academic areas, but it can be used in any content area in which skills can be broken down into specific subareas and target criterion levels can be established.

Domain-Referenced Testing

Domain-Referenced Testing (DRT) is closely related to the criterion-referenced testing approach. The emphasis of the DRT approach, however, is on systematically representing and sampling the specific content, so that a student's performance on a sample of items can be generalized to his/her performance on any other sample of items from the same content area. The steps to this approach are listed below.

1. Describe the basic domain and subdomains and how you arrived at these subdomains.

2. State a terminal objective for the unit. Include the subdomains you have identified.

3. Develop and describe your plan for generating the item pool for each subdomain and your plan for randomly selecting items from this pool for your pretest and posttest.

4. Describe the format of your items. Include this format in your objective. Also indicate how you will record the student's responses.

5. Randomly select items for the pretest and posttest and type up a final copy of each test.

6. Develop an answer key for the pretest and posttest. Also indicate by the item the subdomain to which it corresponds.

7. Develop a scoring grid which groups the items by subdomain. Specify any other scoring and administration procedures.

8. Develop a table for reporting the results of the pretest and posttest by subdomain and total test. This table should have the subdomains across the top and the students' names down the side.

Curriculum-Based Measurement

Curriculum-based measurement (CBM) is an ongoing assessment approach that was developed by individuals at the University of Minnesota.

It consists of a specific set of assessment techniques for the areas of reading, written expression, spelling, and math, using timed samples of the student's work. Norms are usually developed using scores from the local school or district. When using the CBM approach, you would administer probes of short duration to your students on a weekly or twice-weekly basis and graph their performance each week. You would then use the graphic data to evaluate student performance and determine the success of the instructional interventions being used with the students. When students are not progressing, you would change instruction and then examine subsequent data to evaluate the effects of that change (Busch & Espin, 2003).

The majority of the studies on the use of CBM have been at the elementary level. A group of authors, however, has examined the reliability and validity of this approach at the secondary level—in the content areas of reading, written expression, mathematics, social studies, and science (Espin, Busch, Shin, & Kruschwitz, 2001; Espin & Foegen, 1996; Espin et al., 2000: Espin & Tindal, 1998; Tindal & Nolet, 1995).

Portfolio Assessment

The concept of portfolio assessment has been in use in the fine arts area for a number of years, as well as in career and technical education programs such as architecture, drafting, and graphic arts. As the emphasis in assessment moves toward the concept of "authentic assessment," portfolios are being developed in a number of content areas and across content areas. Sitlington and Clark (2006, p. 148) outlined the major steps in portfolio assessment:

- Describe the curricular area
- Identify the overall goals of the portfolio
- Delineate the portfolio format and the type of materials to be included
- Describe procedures for evaluating the work in the portfolio, such as student conferences and teacher review of the material
- Describe how the contents of the portfolio will be summarized

They also identified the following aspects of portfolio assessment as critical to the assessment process (p. 148):

- Criteria for selection of materials must be stated
- Students must participate in the development of these criteria and in the actual selection of the materials
- Criteria for evaluating the materials must be specified
- An opportunity for self-reflection on the part of the student must be provided

The types of materials to be included in the portfolio can range from the results of vocational interest inventories, to essays written by the student concerning his or her goals, to samples of projects from English class or architectural drafting, to results of performance samples. This approach is an excellent method of compiling and summarizing all of the transition assessment activities of the student. In using this method, it is critical that the student have input into the types of materials to be included in the portfolio and that the guidelines that have been established be followed. A portfolio with everything the student has completed will be difficult to evaluate and does not truly represent the student's abilities, interests, and preferences. It is also important that the material in the portfolio be evaluated on an ongoing basis.

Advantages and Disadvantages of Curriculum-Based Assessment

Since the curriculum-based assessment approaches are tied directly to the student's performance in the content being studied, a great deal of information can be gathered through this approach. In addition, curriculum-based assessment is often done naturally by teachers; all that is needed to make this assessment more effective is to pay more attention to the structure of the assessment and to record the results in a systematic way so that others can use them.

Curriculum-based assessment is also becoming a major emphasis within academic content area courses. This presents an ideal opportunity to gather information about the individual across a variety of instructional settings, particularly related to postsecondary education and training. If data are gathered on the student's performance in academic classes, information can be gathered on basic academic skills, how the student learns best, and the student's work habits, preferences and values, and attitudes. The specific academic areas in which the student is interested and in which he or she excels can also be identified. The curriculum-based assessment approach can provide information about the student's performance and/or knowledge of skills related to daily living, such as managing a checking account, negotiating with authority figures, doing laundry, and preparing meals. Finally, this approach can provide information about the student's interests and skills in leisure-time activities.

Curriculum-based assessment approaches also provide the information needed to make appropriate curriculum and instructional modifications. This approach is also one of the best methods of determining the amount of support the student needs in a specific course or program. What better way of determining the support needed than by involving the student in the program and identifying the supports that helped him or her succeed in that program? The disadvantage of curriculum-based assessment is that it is closely tied to the curriculum of the specific school or district. This makes it difficult to compare the performance of students coming from different schools, which some adult service providers may wish to do, as they are making decisions regarding eligibility for their services.

Performance Samples

Performance samples can be used to assess an individual's needs, strengths, preferences, interests, and personal/social characteristics. The key to administering performance samples is that the practitioner observe and document such areas of information as level of interest in the activity, attention to task, and requests for assistance or clarification, in addition to the individual's actual performance of the task. Performance samples can be used to replicate some aspects of career and technical education programs or work environments. Samples of daily activities can also replicate aspects of independent living.

Performance samples generally fall into two categories: commercially made and locally developed. Commercial performance samples are generally found in vocational evaluation units in school systems or rehabilitation facilities. Examples of commercial work samples include Talent Assessment Program (TAP) and Valpar. See Brown, McDaniel, and Couch (1994) for an overview of these commercial systems. In brief, commercial performance samples come with standardized directions, tasks, materials, scoring procedures, and norms that enhance administration procedures. They tend to be expensive to purchase (anywhere from several hundred dollars to several thousand dollars). Commercially available performance samples can also become dated quickly and not reflect work tasks in the local employment sector. Some commercially available performance samples are focused on generic tasks that go across many jobs and do not replicate work directly; therefore, some students may still have the feeling that they are taking a test. Finally, for individuals with physical or severe disabilities, these commercial samples may indicate what they cannot do, as opposed to what they can do if they are given appropriate training and support to learn a task.

Locally developed or homemade work samples are generally developed by a teacher or vocational evaluator. These performance samples can be developed using tasks in career and technical education programs, local jobs, or living options in the community. For example, a teacher could develop a performance sample for individuals to make corsages from plastic or real flowers, based upon a job analysis conducted at a local florist. Students would select floral designs from appropriate books and follow predetermined directions and/or demonstrations to assemble their project. Key behaviors the teacher might observe include level of student interest, eye-hand coordination, attention to detail, artistic ability, and attention span. Follow-up activities may include a visit to a horticulture program within the school system or to a local florist. Information concerning job opportunities, pay, and training needed could be obtained from the Occupational Information Network (O*NET, http://www.doleta.gov/programs/onet/) or from a state occupational information system.

Locally developed performance samples can also be found within vocational evaluation units in schools and tend to sample tasks found in career and technical education programs or jobs specific to the local community. These samples tend to have high face validity, since individuals can see and carry out actual work activities. For example, students may take apart, clean, and put together a carburetor. Key behaviors to observe might include level of interest, spatial relationships, problem-solving strategies, attention to task, memory, eye-hand coordination, and finger dexterity. For students who are interested and do well at the task, follow-up activities might include spending time in the auto mechanics program to observe other activities or shadowing an auto mechanic in the community.

Performance samples generally have a standard set of directions, tasks, materials, and key behaviors to observe. The format for self-developed performance samples typically includes

I. Introduction
   A. Title
   B. Description of performance sample
   C. List of tasks
   D. Vocational or daily living tasks to which sample will relate
   E. Argument for content validity of performance sample

II. Instructions to evaluator
   A. Prerequisite skills
   B. Detailed description of work sample conditions
   C. Directions for setup and breakdown

III. Administration
   A. Directions for individual
   B. Directions for evaluator for instruction and demonstration

IV. Scoring and interpreting the information gathered
   A. Overview of types of information to be collected
   B. Directions and forms for collecting each type of information
   C. Insights into comparing and interpreting the information gathered
   D. Insights into integrating the information gathered into the overall assessment and transition planning process

V. Construction of performance sample
   A. List of materials required for administration
   B. Diagrams or photographs
   C. Instructions for assembly

VI. Additional information (if needed)

Developing informal performance samples can be time consuming and costly for some practitioners. However, they can provide you with a great deal of information about the individual's interests, strengths, and work habits and attitudes, while allowing the individual to explore different areas. It also allows you to provide a controlled environment for the student, as opposed to an actual work or living situation. It is always important to weigh the benefits and limitations of using performance samples as opposed to placing students in actual sites (situational assessments) to perform similar tasks.

Behavioral Observation Techniques

Observing and recording individual behavior in a variety of community living, work, and academic settings is a key aspect of transition assessment. Observing individual behavior is a key component of a number of the methods described in this section. Although behavioral observation is presented here as a separate technique, behavioral observation approaches are often used in gathering information as part of the performance sample approach presented previously and as part of the situational assessment process described in the following section. In all of the following strategies, students should also be asked to give feedback concerning their perceptions of the observed behavior, and the results of the observation should be shared with them.

Strategies for Recording Behavior

For information to be useful, behavior observation should be systematic and should take place in a variety of settings. It is also helpful to have different team members observe the same individual in various situations to make sure the information gathered is valid and reliable. Kerr and Nelson (2006) identified a number of strategies that can be used to observe and record behavior. These strategies are summarized in the following paragraphs. Refer to this or other sources on behavior management for more detailed information.

Permanent Products. This involves recording the number of products produced, with a simple count over a specified amount of time or a number of products per minute or hour.

Frequency. This is the method of choice for most behaviors that are brief and have a definite beginning and end. If observation periods vary in length, you may convert the information to rate per minute by dividing the count by the number of minutes you observed that day.

Number of Trials to a Performance Criterion. This approach allows you to measure the number of trials it takes the student to perform a task he or she has been taught to the accuracy level you have established.

Duration. This method is most useful for behaviors that last a long period of time. Any watch or second hand may be used to record the amount of time the behavior occurs. Although a total duration recording procedure is more convenient, recording the duration per occurrence may be more helpful in describing the same behaviors.

Response Latency. This recording technique involves starting a timer when a verbal or visual request is made and stopping the time when the student complies with the request.

Interval Recording. This approach allows you to record both continuous behaviors, as well as those that have a definite beginning and end. Although it requires your full attention for observing and recording behaviors, you or your aide can observe several behaviors or students at once. This is also a good method for observing behaviors that occur too frequently to be accurately counted separately, such as hand flapping. When using this technique you would break the observation period down into small intervals of equal length (10, 15, or 30 seconds) and record whether the behavior occurred or did not occur during each interval. The size of the interval should be at least as long as the average duration of a single response, but short enough so that two complete responses normally cannot occur in the same interval. To summarize the information you would report the percentage of intervals in which the behavior was observed.

Momentary Time Sampling. This is the most useful approach if you do not have a block of time to devote to observing and recording behavior, want to sample behaviors across an extended time period, or want to monitor a number of students. In this approach you would rate the occurrence or nonoccurrence of the behavior at each specific time your observe. Watch timers, kitchen timers, or recorded tapes with sounds set to specific intervals can be used in this approach. To avoid students predicting when the next observation will occur, it is best to set the observation times at different intervals. This approach is one of the most useful for involving students in the recording of their own behaviors. The major drawback to this method is that behaviors occurring away from the observation time are not recorded.

Summary. The key to using the behavioral observation approach effectively is to (a) clearly define the behavior to be observed, so that different people observing the behavior at the same time would record the same results; (b) select the observation method that will most accurately reflect the occurrence of the behavior but still be something you can carry out; (c) determine the amount of time each day for the observation and for how many days the observation will continue; and (d) decide who is in the best position to conduct the observation.

Finally, it is very important that the student be involved in the observation process and that the results be shared with the student. Often, having students "count" their behavior as you are counting it allows them to see for the themselves the extent of their behavior.

Rating Scales

The use of rating scales and checklists allows you to identify the positive behaviors you want to observe and systematically record whether the student is demonstrating those behaviors. Checklists allow you to record whether or not the behavior occurred (yes/no); rating scales allow you to rate the student along a continuum (e.g., *acceptable/unacceptable/needs improvement*, on a 5-point scale). This continuum is an excellent way to show student growth across a number of ratings. We will focus here on the development of rating scales. Many of the points we make, however, also apply to the development of checklists.

Rating scales can be developed locally or obtained from books, manuals, and other assessment materials. Rating scales can save practitioners valuable time, especially when observing a number of individuals in similar situations. They also allow a number of different staff members to be involved in the rating at different times—still focusing on the same behaviors. For example, the practitioners use the same rating scale to determine whether students can successfully use public transportation to the local recreation center. The rating scale includes such items as (a) identifies the appropriate bus, (b) states what time the bus leaves according to the schedule, (c) carries appropriate money for a roundtrip ticket, and (d) identifies the location of the bus pick-up and drop-off. Students can also be asked to rate themselves and provide additional feedback on specific target behaviors.

The actual items selected for the rating scale need to be relevant to specific situations and are dependent on the process and people that developed the scale. In addition, some people tend to rate individuals as being "in the middle" when using rating scales. Therefore, it is necessary to understand the importance of the items on the scale and to observe individuals for enough time that you are confident about your rating.

We propose the following basic rules for developing rating scales:

- Include space for basic information such as student's and rater's names, rater's position, and observation date.
- Decide on odd or even number of response choices.
- Decide whether or not to group items with similar content together.
- Allow space for comments after each item.
- Allow space for comments at end of scale.
- Write specific directions, including the purpose of the scale and how to complete it.
- Put labels at top of response choices (on every page).

Situational Assessment

Situational assessment is a systematic observation process for evaluating behaviors in sites as close as possible to the adult living, working, and educational environments the student has identified. Situational assessments can be a valid and reliable source of data if the sites are systematically developed (e.g., uniform tasks a student will do, amount of time, supervision responsibilities) and if practitioners systematically record behaviors during the assessment process. The data collected then can be used in planning and placement decisions concerning further situational assessment sites, types of programs to consider for placement, and instructional/social accommodations needed in specific situations. The following sections provide examples of situational assessment in different settings.

Situational Assessment for the Transition to Work

Situational assessment can be used to collect data on students' interests, abilities, social/interpersonal skills, and accommodations/needs in school-based work sites, community-based work sites, and career and technical education programs. The following examples illustrate two situational assessment sites:

A tenth-grade student has repeatedly expressed an interest in enrolling in a welding program. The teacher arranges for the individual to spend a week in a career and technical education welding program to determine interest level, ability to follow safety rules, ability to use the equipment and tools required in the program, interactions with the instructor and other students, and what (if any) instructional and/or equipment accommodations would be needed. Both the welding instructor and the transition teacher agree to collect narrative data on a daily basis in addition to using a competency-based checklist of tasks the individual completed while in the program. At the end of the assessment, the instructor, teacher, and student discuss whether this is a realistic placement option and/or postsecondary employment goal for the student.

An eighth-grade student is placed in the library for an in-school situational assessment. The purpose of the assessment is for career exploration and observation of the individual's work and social skills. The librarian and teacher determine that the student will check out books, return books to shelves, and repair torn and damaged books. The teacher observes the student's social interactions at the check-out desk, ability to catalog books alphabetically and numerically, and ability to work independently repairing books on an intermittent basis three weeks. The librarian agrees to supplement these data with information concerning the student's interest level, attention to task, and social interaction. At the end of the situational assessment, the librarian, teacher, and student discuss the student's strengths, needs, preferences, and interests noted throughout the assessment. Additional in-school work sites are then discussed to further the career exploration process.

In arranging situational assessments in work sites, educators should also keep in mind that guidelines have been developed by the U.S.

Departments of Labor and Education for the purpose of placing students in unpaid job sites while meeting the requirements of the Fair Labor Standards Act (Pumpian, Fisher, Certo, Engel, & Mautz, 1998; Simon & Halloran, 1994). In brief, the guidelines state that participation in unpaid work sites must be for vocational exploration, assessment, or training in a community-based work site under the supervision of public school personnel. Community-based placements must be clearly defined in the IEP, along with a statement of needed transition services established for the purposes of exploration, assessment, training, or cooperative education.

Situational Assessment for the Transition to Life in the Community

As illustrated below, situational assessments can also be conducted in recreation sites, community sites (e.g. use of a bank facility), and simulated or real sites that require independent living skills (e.g., home economics lab, family home).

A student participates in an afterschool soccer team. The teacher observes the student's interactions with teammates and the coach. Also noted is the student's interest in the game and ability to follow directions. The teacher, student, and family can explore additional recreation opportunities in the community based on these initial assessment data.

Situational Assessment for the Transition to Postsecondary Education

Situational assessments related to the transition to postsecondary education should take place on the campus of the type of postsecondary institution the student is thinking of attending. Such an assessment might look like this.

José is thinking of attending a major university in the state. He and his parents contact this university to arrange for a campus visit. During this visit, they are given a tour of the campus. Most important, though, José is allowed to accompany a student ambassador for the student's entire college day. This includes attending classes with the student and also spending the night in the dorm. Before the visit, José and his teacher sit down and draft a list of questions for José to ask, along with a list of things José should observe during his time on campus. While he is on the visit, José takes notes, using this list of questions. Following the visit, José types up his notes, and then meets with his teacher to discuss this information.

Advantages and Disadvantages of Situational Assessment

The advantages of using situational assessment as an integral part of transition assessment include that individuals are exposed to actual community, work, or educational environments, can participate in real tasks in real environments, and are able to interact with peers and adults with and without disabilities. It can also be used to motivate individuals to explore a range of interests in community, leisure, work, and postsecondary education settings. Practitioners can document strengths and needs across settings and use the information in the transition planning process. Another advantage of situational assessment is that the information is being collected while the student is in an actual living, working, or education setting as close as possible to where he or she sees herself in adult life. Unlike performance samples, however, the environment in situational assessments cannot be controlled, and the emphasis is not as much on teaching specific skills before they are assessed. Practitioners should also note that situational assessments require coordination with school personnel, community personnel, employers, and family members. A situational assessment must be well planned and include systematic recording of behavior. This information should then be used to plan further situational assessments or make recommendations for placement and support in similar settings.

Being Sensitive to Gender and Cultural Diversity

Across all of the assessment techniques presented in the previous sections, you must always be sensitive to issues of gender and cultural diversity. The number one issue in gender and cultural sensitivity is fairness. Common-sense sensitivity to gender and cultural factors in selecting standardized instruments, developing informal procedures, and interpreting and reporting assessment results will ordinarily not only conform to federal mandates for nondiscriminatory evaluation but also go beyond them. Clark (2007) stated some common-sense guidelines that are summarized here:

- Be aware of possible past discrimination in the assessment process.
- Be ready to respond positively to identified past discrimination experiences. This may involve assigning a same-gender, same-race, same-language, or same-ethnic-group professional to conduct the assessment and provide appropriate interpretations and reports.
- When in doubt about the proper interpretations to be made from a student or family response in the assessment process, use selected members of their cultural community to verify impressions or clarify responses that are difficult to understand.
- When interviewing a student or family of a different cultural group for the first time, be careful about the use of names and titles. Attempting to be friendly too quickly may be insulting and viewed as a violation of social etiquette.
- Talk with the student and family about the best way to communicate, then be sure that comprehension is working both ways in the

process by summarizing what has been said or by asking the student or family member to summarize what has been said.

- If translators (for written materials) or interpreters (for oral interactions) are requested and used, spend time with them before their participation to acquaint them with the purpose and context of the assessment activity.

As Sitlington and Clark (2006) pointed out, planning for life transitions requires a proactive level of thinking that is associated with middle-class people. These individuals often have education, economic security, and relatively high levels of success in their own life transitions. To many students with disabilities and their families, transition planning is an unfamiliar concept and beyond their current concerns for day-to-day survival. The language used in talking about transitions in assessment activities (e.g., *vision for the future, empowerment, independence/interdependence, self-determination*, etc.) may be difficult for them to understand. Even if they have no difficulty understanding the words, they might have different cultural values associated with the words. Be sensitive to communication barriers and work continuously to establish common understandings when performing student and parent assessments and use those common understandings when drafting IEP goals and objectives.

Summary of Methods of Gathering Information About the Individual

The preceding sections have identified a number of methods of gathering information about the individual to be used in the transition planning process. The best way to determine which methods would be useful to you at a specific phase of the transition assessment process is to determine the questions you need to answer regarding the student and the information you need to answer these questions. You, in cooperation with the student and others on the planning team, can then choose the methods that can provide the information you need. The portfolio approach presented earlier in this chapter offers an ideal vehicle for the student, family, and other members of the transition planning team to select and compile the most relevant transition assessment information that has been collected. This transition assessment portfolio can then be used in making the match between the student's needs, strengths, preferences and interests, and the future environments in which the student will function as an adult.

It is critical that the information gathered through the transition assessment process be used to drive the IEP and develop the course of study for the student. Transition assessment information is also critical in developing the student's Summary of Performance.

METHODS OF ASSESSING POTENTIAL ENVIRONMENTS

The first section of this chapter presented information about a number of methods for gathering information about the student. To make a match between the student's strengths and interests and future environments, however, you also need to have information about the demands of the living, working, and educational environments in which the student will be functioning as an adult and the educational programs in which the student will enroll on the way to adulthood. Analysis of these environments also entails examining circumstances and situations that occur within these environments.

In order to determine the preparation and support the student will need to succeed in the future living, working, and educational environments he or she has identified, it is critical that the student, you, or someone in your program systematically look at the demands of these environments. This process can range from simple to complex, depending upon the environment being studied and the level of functioning of the student. In general, the lower-functioning the student (or the bigger you feel the gap will be between the student's abilities and the demands of the environment), the more detailed the analysis should be. This will allow you to identify the needed education and supports that the student will need to succeed.

The concept of universal design in all environments assists in the transition of youth with disabilities to all living, working, and educational environments. This concept originated in the field of architecture, when architects realized that by considering the needs of their buildings' potential users at the outset, they could subtly integrate universal accessibility into the fabric of the building's design. As this concept of access for all spread to areas such as civic engineering and commercial product design, it was found that addressing the divergent needs of special populations increased usability for everyone. In the same way, the concept of universal design for learning has at its core the idea that all curriculum materials should be designed from the outset of instruction in order to teach all students effectively (Pisha & Coyne, 2001; Rose & Meyer, 2002).

It is important to remember that the environment, situations, and circumstances can be adapted, adjusted, or realigned so that minimal supports will be needed. The following section presents basic information about analyzing community settings, work environments, and postsecondary training programs. Although the focus of this chapter is on analyzing future environments, the same techniques can be used to analyze the current environments in which the student is living, working, and going to school.

Analysis of Community Environments

The concept of environmental analysis, particularly related to community-based living settings, was first introduced by professionals working with individuals with severe disabilities. In terms of future living environments, it is important to identify the demands of both the home environment in which the individual will be living and the immediate and broader community in which the individual will be shopping, banking, and pursuing leisure activities.

Alper (2003) proposed the following steps in identifying curricular content using the ecological inventory approach:

- Select the domain to be considered (e.g., domestic).
- Identify environments within the domain in which the student needs to learn to function (e.g., home).
- Identify subenvironments that are a priority for the student (e.g., kitchen, family room).
- Identify activities within each subenvironment in which the student is to be included (e.g., heating up leftovers, operating the DVD player).
- Task analyze the priority activities into their component skills.

If the specific community-based environments are known, the task becomes one of analyzing the demands of these specific environments (e.g., the apartment, the grocery store, the bank). Often, however, we do not know the specific location in which the individual will be living. In addition, the individual will want to frequent a number of locations within a given community, such as a number of different restaurants. For this reason McDonnell, Wilcox, and Hardman (1991) recommended a "general case procedures" analysis in which you identify the variations in performance demands across all of the settings in which the individual will be expected to complete each activity. There are six steps in performing such a general case analysis. The steps will need to be outlined in much more detail for individuals with more severe disabilities than for those with mild disabilities. We will use the example of using an ATM card to make a cash withdrawal at an ATM machine.

- Define the environments in which the individual will be expected to perform the activity, the tasks the individual will complete at the sites, when the individual will be expected to use the settings, and how the individual will meet the performance demands of the activity. (Identify the types of ATM machines in the community, when the individual might use them, and whether the individual will use the machine alone or with assistance.)
- Identify the sequence of generic response steps required to complete the activity. (List the basic steps the individual must perform in using a typical ATM machine.)
- Identify generic environmental cues for each response in the activity. (Identify the prompts given by a typical ATM machine for each step identified in Item 2.)

- Record variation in the generic environmental cues across performance sites. (List the variations in the prompts that are given by the different types of ATM machines in the community.)
- Record variation in the generic responses of the activity. (List the variations in the responses the individual must make to the different types of ATM machines in the community.)
- Identify exceptions in the performance universe. (Identify ATM machines in the community in which there are major differences in the prompts given by the machine or the steps the individual must follow. Decide whether it is important for the individual to learn to deal with these exceptions.)

A sample form for completing an analysis of the community environment is provided in Appendix C. This form focuses on gathering information about a number of components of the community including community resources, services for individuals with disabilities, employment resources, postsecondary education programs, independent living support providers, and transportation services.

Analysis of Work Environments

The process of analyzing the demands of working environments is called *job analysis.* In essence, it is a task analysis of the job and of the demands of the job, as well as the culture of the workplace. This process involves systematically gathering information about what the worker does and how the work is done. This includes other areas such as amount of supervision, production requirements, and so forth. Information should also be gathered on other demands of the workplace, including activities during breaks and transportation to and from work.

Rogan, Grossi, and Gajewski (2002) identified four major focal points for an ecological inventory and workplace analysis:

- Physical environment (accessibility, layout)
- Typical activities or work tasks (rate, sequence, quality, frequency, duration)
- People within the environment (age, gender, characteristics of supervisors and coworkers, nature of interactions)
- Climate and culture (customs, traditions, rituals, routines, rules, expectations)

We will use the example of a dental assistant.

- Identify the specific responses that will be required to complete each job assigned. These responses should be both observable and measurable. (Identify the basic tasks that the dental assistant must complete. Be very specific. Identify the tasks you have observed and other tasks completed at a time you weren't observing.)

- Identify the environmental cues that will control the completion of the task. These will be cues to tell the individual to perform certain tasks or certain parts of the task. (Identify the commands of the dentist, the requests of the patient, and the requests of other office staff that prompt the specific tasks.)
- Identify the speed requirements of the job in terms of average time required to complete a response or task or number of products to be completed within a given time period. Identify how important this speed requirement is to the employer. (Identify how quickly the dental assistant must respond to the requests of the dentist, patient, and other staff. Indicate how important speed is.)
- Specify the quality requirements for each job task. The accuracy of the supervisor's expectations should be cross-checked by discussing them with coworkers who perform the same job. (Identify what criteria will be used to evaluate the quality of the dental assistant's performance.)
- Identify exceptions to the normal routine. These exceptions may include changes in the job routine or unpredictable situations that may arise during the course of the workday. (Identify tasks the dental assistant does not perform daily but that are important to completion of the job.)

A sample job analysis form is provided in Appendix D. It is important for you to identify the types of information you want to gather on a job and adopt, adapt, or develop a job analysis form that will provide this information for you. The form should allow you to record information about a specific job, as well as comments you want to make. The form should also be one that all staff members can use and that will allow the results of a specific job analysis to be shared with other staff and the individual. Regardless of the form that you use, be sure to specifically identify the (a) specific tasks of the job, (b) basic academic skills needed (reading, math, written and oral communication), and (c) social skills, work habits, and attitudes required by the job. In this process it is important to directly observe the worker and to talk with the worker and direct supervisor. Also check to see if there is an existing job description that has been developed by the employer that can help with your analysis.

Analysis of Postsecondary Education Environments

If one of the goals of the student is postsecondary education, you, the student, and/or the family should visit the targeted educational program to determine the demands of specific courses and of the total educational environment. This involves gathering information about the specific courses in which the student will be enrolled and determining the demands of these courses in terms of such aspects as daily assignments, amount of reading required, and major tests. Information should also be gathered on the requirements of any field experiences or laboratories related to the class. In addition, you should identify the support services and accommodations that are available.

Information should be gathered on the following aspects of the program: (a) application procedures; (b) admission procedures; (c) support services and willingness of individual faculty members to provide accommodations; (d) career/personal counseling services; (e) training programs, both academically and vocationally related; (f) existing fee structure; and (g) availability of financial support. As with the job analysis form, it is important for you to identify the types of information you want to gather on postsecondary programs and adopt, adapt, or develop a program analysis form that will provide this information for you. The form should allow you to record information about a specific program and then refer to this information at a later date. The form should also be one that all staff members can use and that will allow the results of a specific program analysis to be shared with other staff and the individual.

A sample program analysis form for a career and technical education program is provided in Appendix E. The first part of this form focuses on gathering information about the institution as a whole and the programs and support services offered. The second part of the form focuses on the specific career and technical program in which the student is interested.

Analysis of Secondary Education Programs

An analysis of the future living, working, and educational environments the individual has chosen will be a major help in determining the instruction he or she will need to succeed in these programs. This preparation could involve enrollment in general education courses in high school, participating in work experiences in the community, instruction in learning strategies or study skills, or instruction in self-determination. It will be helpful to conduct an analysis of the demands of these secondary education programs so that you can determine the support the student will need in order to learn from these programs. The steps involved in this program analysis are identical to those discussed in analyzing postsecondary educational environments. Noting the supports and accommodations that proved useful for the student in these programs will be helpful in determining the supports and accommodations needed as a young adult.

SUMMARY

This chapter provided an overview of methods you can use to collect assessment data throughout the transition planning process. There are a number of methods that can provide information about the individual in terms of needs, preferences and interests, past experiences, and future plans. Each of these methods provides different types of information. It is important to determine (a) the questions that need to be answered and (b) the information you need in order to answer these questions. You should then select the methods that do the best job of providing this information. Selection of the specific methods used in the assessment process should also be aligned with the specific goals, interests, and preferences of the student. If a student chooses not to participate in a specific aspect of the assessment, this choice should be honored. The reason for the student's decision should also be noted.

It is also important to gather information about the demands of the living, working, and educational environments the individual has identified. Information related to these areas should include the demands of these environments and the supports (both natural and more formal) that are available for the individual within these environments. Information should also be gathered on the demands of secondary-level programs that will be needed to prepare the individual for these future environments.

Once information has been gathered related to the individual and the future living, working, and educational environments, it is critical to combine this information to determine the best match between the individual and future environments and the support the individual will need to succeed in these environments. It is also important to continually update this information. Chapter 7 presents information that will help you, the student, and the family make this match.

REFERENCES

Alper, S. (2003). An ecological approach to identifying curriculum content for inclusive settings. In D. L. Ryndak & S. Alper, *Curriculum and instruction for students with significant disabilities in inclusive settings* (2nd ed.) (pp. 73–85). Boston: Allyn & Bacon.

Brown, C. D., McDaniel, R., & Couch, R. (1994). *Vocational evaluation systems and software: A consumer's guide.* Menomonie, WI: Rehabilitation Resource, Stout Vocational Rehabilitation Institute.

Busch, T. W., & Espin, C. A. (2003). Using curriculum-based measurement to prevent failure and assess learning in the content areas. *Assessment for Effective Intervention, 28*(3&4), 49–58.

Clark, G. M. (2007). *Assessment for transitions planning* (2nd ed.). Austin, TX: Pro-Ed.

Espin, C. A., Busch, T. W., Shin, J., & Kruschwitz, R. (2001). Curriculum-based measures in the content areas: Validity of vocabulary-matching as an indicator of performance in a social studies classroom. *Learning Disabilities Research and Practice, 16,* 142–151.

Espin, C. A., & Foegen, A. (1996). Validity of general outcome measures for predicting secondary students' performance on content-area tasks. *Exceptional Children, 62*(6), 497–514.

Espin, C. A., Skare, S., Shin, J., Deno, S. L., Robinson, S., & Brenner, B. (2000). Identifying indicators of growth in written expression for middle-school students. *Journal of Special Education, 34*, 140–153.

Espin, C. A., & Tindal, G. (1998). Curriculum-based measurement for secondary students. In M. R. Shinn, (Ed.), *Advanced applications of curriculum-based measurement*. New York: Guilford.

Individuals with Disabilities Education Improvement Act of 2004, 20 U.S.C. § 1400 (2004).

Kerr, M. M., & Nelson, C. H. (2006). *Strategies for addressing behavior problems in the classroom* (5th ed.). Upper Saddle River, NJ: Merrill-Prentice Hall.

McDonnell, J., Wilcox, B., & Hardman, M. (1991). *Secondary programs for students with developmental disabilities.* Boston: Allyn & Bacon.

Neubert, D. A., & Moon, M. S. (2000). How a transition profile helps students prepare for life in the community. *Teaching Exceptional Children, 32*(2), 20–25.

Pisha, B., & Coyne, P. (2001). Smart from the start: The promise of universal design for learning. *Remedial and Special Education, 22*(4), 197–203.

Pumpian, I., Fisher, D., Certo, N. J., Engel, T., & Mautz, D. (1998). To pay or not to pay: Differentiating employment and training relationships through regulation and litigation. *Career Development for Exceptional Individuals, 21*, 187–202.

Rogan, P., Grossi, T. A., & Gajewski, R. (2002). Vocational and career assessment. In C. L. Sax & C. A. Thoma, *Transition assessment: Wise practices for quality lives* (pp. 103–117). Baltimore: Paul H. Brookes.

Rose, D. H. & Meyer, A. (2002). *Teaching every student in the digital age: Universal design for learning.* Alexandria, VA: Association for Supervision and Curriculum Development.

Salvia, J., & Ysseldyke, J. E. (2004). *Assessment in special education and inclusive education* (9th ed.). Boston: Houghton Mifflin.

Sax, C. L. (2002). Person-centered planning: More than a strategy. In C. L. Sax & C. A. Thoma, *Transition assessment: Wise practices for quality lives* (pp. 13–24). Baltimore: Paul H. Brookes.

Schwartz, A. A., Holburn, S. C., & Jacobson, J. W. (2000). Defining person-centeredness: Results of two consensus methods. *Education and Training in Mental Retardation and Developmental Disabilities, 35*(3), 235–249.

Simon, M., & Halloran, W. (1994). Community-based vocational education: Guidelines for complying with the Fair Labor Standards Act. *Journal of the Association for Severely Handicapped, 19*, 52–60.

Sitlington, P. L., & Clark, G. M. (2006). *Transition education and services for students with disabilities* (4th ed.). Boston: Allyn & Bacon.

Sitlington, P. L., Neubert, D. A., & Leconte, P. J. (1997). Transition assessment: The position of the Division on Career Development and Transition. *Career Development for Exceptional Individuals, 20*(1), 69–79.

Tindal, G., & Nolet, V. (1995). Curriculum-based measurement in middle and high schools: Critical thinking skills in content areas. *Focus on Exceptional Children, 27*(7), 1–22.

Whitfield, E. A., Feller, R. W., & Wood, C. (2007). *A counselor's guide to career assessment instruments, 5th ed.* Columbus, OH: National Career Development Association.

ADDITIONAL RESOURCES

Clark, G. M. (2007). *Assessment for transitions planning.* Austin, TX: Pro Ed.

Clark, G. M., Patton, J. R., & Moulton, L. R. (2000). *Informal assessments for transition planning.* Austin, TX: Pro-Ed.

Miller, R. J., Lombard, R. C., & Corbey, S. A. (2007). *Transition assessment: Planning transition and IEP development for youth with mild to moderate disabilities.* Boston: Allyn & Bacon.

Neubert, D. A. (2003). The role of assessment in the transition to adult life process for individuals with disabilities. *Exceptionality, 11,* 63–71.

Sax, C. L., & Thoma, C. A. (2002). *Transition assessment: Wise practices for quality lives.* Baltimore: Paul H. Brookes.

Sitlington, P. L., & Payne, E. M. (2004). Information needed by postsecondary education: Can we provide it as part of the transition assessment process? *Learning Disabilities: A Contemporary Journal, 2*(2), 1–14.

Matching Students to Environments

Making Transition Assessment a Success

This chapter presents transition assessment as an ongoing process with the goal of gathering information about the student and his or her current and future living, working, and educational environments. The end goal of this process is to use this information to make the best match possible between the student and environments he or she has identified. The goals of this chapter are to

- Outline the transition assessment process for making the best match between the student's needs, strengths, preferences, and interests, and the demands of current and future living, working, and educational environments
- Describe the steps in developing an assessment plan for gathering the information to answer these questions

THE TRANSITION ASSESSMENT PROCESS

The three major components of the transition assessment are presented in Figure 7.1 and each is briefly explained.

Figure 7.1   Transition Assessment: Matching for Success

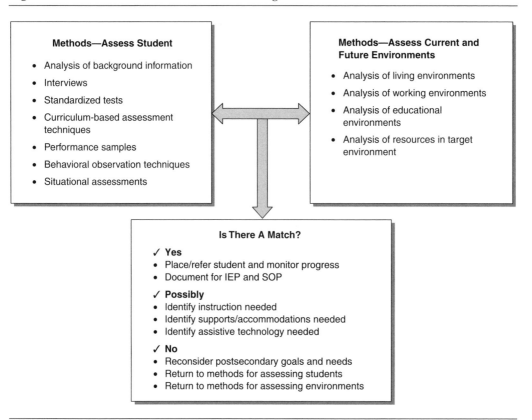

Assess the Student

The first step is to identify the student's needs, strengths, preferences, and interests through a variety of assessment methods. This step should be carried out using a combination of the methods presented in Chapter 6 and individualized for each student. These methods include analysis of background information, interviews, standardized tests, curriculum-based assessment techniques, performance samples, behavior observation techniques, and situational assessments.

Assess Environments

The second step is to identify and analyze the current and future living, working, and educational environments of interest to the student. It is necessary to determine the demands and characteristics of these environments. A variety of methods can help to accomplish this (see sample forms in Appendices C, D, and E and refer to Chapter 6 for a review of these methods). For example, if the student is interested in working, a job analysis should be conducted to determine the essential functions of the job and the supports available in this environment. A formal support might be a job coach from an adult service provider. A natural support might be a co-worker who reminds the student about breaks and lunchtime. It is also important to consider the social/personal relationships (or the workplace culture) present in the immediate and surrounding environment. For example, how do people dress? Is the environment relaxed and friendly or formal and structured?

Make the Match

Once information has been gathered about the student and potential environments it is time to compare the student's needs, strengths, preferences, and interests with the demands of the target environment. In determining if there is a match, you will take one of three routes with the student, family, and other planning team members. If there appears to be a good match between the student and the target environment, make the placement or referral and monitor the progress of the student. If a match is possible, but not definite, identify the accommodations, supports, assistive technology, and/or interagency resources the student will need to succeed in the environment. You may also consider if the student needs more instruction either before being placed in the environment or after being placed in the environment. Finally, if the student and the other IEP team members determine there is not a good match even with supports, accommodations, or assistive technology, it will be necessary to continue to collect information about the student's needs, strengths, preferences, and interests, and the demands of other living, working, and educational environments. This information should be collected as quickly as possible, and the matching process should be initiated again. The following case study illustrates this matching process.

Case Study 1

Rosa is a sophomore in high school. At her IEP meeting, which was held in the spring, she indicated that she would like to be a graphic artist. Her parents supported this goal, but neither they nor Rosa knew exactly what training would be needed or what the job would demand. The IEP team (including Rosa and her parents) designed an assessment plan to be implemented during her junior year. This plan would assist Rosa in gathering information about her needs, taking into account her strengths, preferences, and interests. This plan also indicated the information that would need to be gathered about the job of graphic artist, postsecondary education programs, and residential options available with these programs.

Rosa asked the team to compile information from her previous records and to interview her art teacher and her parents. She also asked that someone observe her in her art class and review a portfolio of her artwork that she had been putting together since junior high school. In addition, she spent two days participating in the graphic arts class at the local community college.

To gather information about the demands of the job, Rosa interviewed three graphic artists in town and spent a day shadowing each worker. She also consulted O*NET to read the tasks included under the graphic artist occupation. Rosa decided that she wanted to attend a community college in the southern part of the state, so she could live away from home. She and her parents visited the graphic arts program at this college. They also talked with the director of services for students with disabilities to determine the support services that would be available to assist Rosa with the reading demands of the classes. They also asked about the natural supports other students might be willing to give Rosa if she had questions or needed help in taking notes and about what types of universal design were used in the courses.

In addition to gathering information about the instructional program, Rosa and her parents visited the apartments right off the campus where most of the students who were not commuters lived. They identified the skills Rosa would need to live by herself or with a roommate in these apartments. Since the local bus served these apartments, Rosa decided that she would not need a car at this time.

The IEP team was called together at the end of the first semester of Rosa's junior year to share the information that had been gathered about Rosa and on the job of graphic artist, the instructional program, and the apartment in which Rosa would be living. They decided that there would be a match between Rosa's strengths, interests, and preferences and the future education and living environments she had identified. Rosa decided that she could succeed in the graphic arts program but that she would use the support services provided by the college. She also decided that she needed to work hard on developing the daily living skills she would need to live on her own, such as balancing a checkbook, budgeting, cooking, and maintaining her apartment. She also indicated that she would need to work more on developing friendships in new situations and asked that her teachers give her some techniques to develop new friendships.

DEVELOPING AN ASSESSMENT PLAN

Chapter 6 provided an overview of methods that can be used to assess the student and analyze living, working, and educational environments in which the student may function as an adult. An obvious challenge is deciding which methods are appropriate at different stages of transition planning and for different students. We suggest that the IEP team develop an assessment plan with the student and the family. This plan can be updated yearly (e.g., for IEP meetings, to determine a course of study for high school) or as the need arises (e.g., student identifies a job of interest in the community, student needs support services from adult service provider after exiting school). The following five questions can be used to develop an assessment plan.

What do I know about this student that would be helpful in developing the assessment plan?

First, review background information about the student. This includes information from previous assessments, medical considerations, previous work history, needs and accommodations, and strengths, preferences, and interests. Second, conduct interviews with the student and family to determine their preferences and goals concerning postschool outcomes. Third, interview other personnel who have been involved with the student concerning the student's needs, strengths, preferences, and interests. At this point it might be helpful to develop a one-page profile of the information you have about the student.

What assessment questions need to be asked and answered for this student during transition assessment?

It is important to find out whether the student has identified postsecondary goals and future environments in which he or she would like to live, learn, and work. Figure 7.2 provides a list of sample questions related to five areas necessary for transition planning: employment, postsecondary education, community involvement, independent living, and social/personal outcomes. These are obviously not all of the questions that could be asked, and the same questions should not be asked of all students, since transition assessment is an ongoing and individualized process. The assessment questions chosen should be triggered by the current and future living, working, and educational environments that the student and his or her family have identified and by the personal/social relationships desired by the student and family. If the student cannot identify goals or future environments at this time, choose questions that will require the student to investigate areas of interest. Some of the questions will remain constant throughout the transition assessment process, but the responses should become more specific. Other questions will arise, however, as the student progresses through school. Early in the process, the interests and preferences of a student will probably be broad, as will future living, working, and educational environments (e.g., I want to go to college). As the student's goals become more focused over time, the future environments identified should also be more specific (e.g., I want to go to college at the state university and will need support services for taking notes and tests).

(Text continues on page 121)

Figure 7.2   Sample Questions to Ask During Transition Assessment

Employment	Need this? No Yes	Methods to Collect Data

1. Does the student have a career or employment goal?	— —	• Interview - student, family
		• Person-Centered Planning
		• Background review
		  IEP
		  Career plan/portfolio
		  Résumé
		• Vocational assessment records

2. What are the student's interests, preferences, and strengths in relation to work?	— —	• Interest inventory
		• Worker preference inventory
		• Work samples
		• Learning style inventories
		• Interview - student, family,
		• Interview - school personnel
		• Situational assessment
		  In-school jobs
		  Career/technology courses
		  Community-based jobs
		  Volunteer/service learning

3. What are the student's needs in terms of support and accommodations on the job?	— —	• Interview - student, family
		• Interview - work-study coordinator
		• Interview - career technology teacher
		• Person-Centered Planning
		• Situational assessment
		  Observation at job sites
		• Record review
		  Vocational experience
		  Accommodations on IEP
		• Assistive technology assessment

4. Can the student state his or her needs and request accommodations on the job if needed?	— —	• Interview - student
		• Interview - employer
		• Interview - work-study coordinator
		• Self-determination assessment
		• Situational assessment
		  Observe in career tech course
		  Observe at job sites

5. Does the student have job-seeking skills (filling out applications, interviewing)?	— —	• Review records
		  Career portfolio
		  Functional academics
		• Interview - student
		• Interview - teachers, guidance
		• Situational assessment
		  Observe in mock interview

6. What types of skills does the student need to acquire or learn in order to meet their career objective?	— —	• Postsecondary program analysis • Job analysis • Career technology program analysis
7. Will the student need support from an adult service provider for competitive or supported employment?	— —	• Interview - student, family • Interview - case manager, teacher • Person-Centered Planning • Background review

Employment	Need this? No Yes	Methods to Collect Data

		Medical review
		IEP - grades, diploma option
		Adaptive behavior assessments
		• Situational assessment
		   Observation at job sites
		• Community analysis (adult
		   services)

8. Does the student receive Supplemental Security Insurance (SSI)?	___ ___	• Interview - student, family • Interview - case manager, teacher • Person-Centered planning • Background review Medical review
9. What types of financial issues (e.g., food stamps, housing subsidies, transportation costs) need to be considered when planning for employment?	___ ___	• Interview - student, family • Interview - case manager, teacher • Person-Centered Planning • Background review Medical review
10. What types of job benefits does the student need in order to become an independent member of society?	___ ___	• Interview - student, family • Interview - case manager, teacher • Person-Centered Planning
Postsecondary Education	Need this? No Yes	Methods to Collect Data

1. Does the student want or need postsecondary education (e.g., college, technical training, adult and continuing education) to reach his or her career or employment goal?	___ ___	• Interview - student, family
		• Interest inventory
		• Person-Centered Planning
		• Record review
		   Vocational experience
		   Accommodations on IEP
		• Situational assessment in stated
		   area of interest

2. Can the student relate his or her interests, preferences, and strengths to a postsecondary education goal?	___ ___	• Interview - student, family
		• Interview - work-study coordinator
		• Interview - career technology
		   teacher
		• Person-Centered Planning
		• Situational assessment
		   Observation at job sites
		• Record review
		   Vocational experience
		   Interests, preferences on IEP

3. What subject(s) or major does the student intend to pursue?	___ ___	• Interview - student, family
		• Interest inventory
		• Interview - career technology
		   teacher
		• Situational assessment in stated
		   areas of interest

(Continued)

Figure 7.2 (Continued)

Postsecondary Education	Need this? No	Yes	Methods to Collect Data
4. What types of accommodations will the student need in a postsecondary setting?	___	___	• Interview - student, family • Background review IEP • Assessment of study skills and time management skills • Assessment of needs in precollege program
5. Are there assistive technology devices that will support the student's participation in postsecondary education classes and/or campus life?	___	___	• Interview - student, family • Observation in general education and/or the community • Assistive technology assessment
6. Can the student express his or her need for support services and/or accommodations if needed?	___	___	• Interview - student, family • Interview - general educator • Person-Centered Planning • Observation at IEP meetings and in general education classes
7. Does the student need assistance in selecting an institution or completing applications forms?	___	___	• Interview - student, family • Interview - teachers, guidance • Person-Centered Planning • Simulated application package • Community analysis
8. Does the student need financial assistance to attend a postsecondary institution?	___	___	• Interview - student, family • Interview - teachers, guidance • Person-Centered Planning • Simulated application package
Community Involvement	Need this? No	Yes	Methods to Collect Data
1. What public transportation is available to the student in his or her community?	___	___	• Community analysis • Interview - student, family • Interview - work-study coordinator
2. Is the student able to use public transportation if available?	___	___	• Interview - student • Situational assessment - public transportation
3. Does the student have a driver's license or need assistance in preparing for a driver's license?	___	___	• Interview - student, family • Record review
4. Does the student need financial assistance from a community agency to access transportation?	___	___	• Interview - student, family • Interview - case manager • Record review
5. Does the student need special travel arrangements made on an ongoing basis to get to work or leisure activities?	___	___	• Interview - student, family • Record review • Situational assessment in community

Community Involvement	Need this? No Yes	Methods to Collect Data
6. Does the student need assistive technology in order to use public transportation or drive (e.g., van equipped with lift)?	___ ___	• Interview - student, family • Interview - case manager • Situational assessment Public transportation

7. What leisure/community activities does the student enjoy?	___ ___	• Interview - student, family
		• Interview - teachers
		• Background review
		    IEP
		• Situational assessment
		    Extracurricular activities
		    Community activities

8. What accommodations does the student need to participate in leisure activities?	___ ___	• Interview - student, family
		• Background review - IEP
		• Situational assessment
		    Physical education classes
		    Extracurricular activities

9. Can the student locate/use community services such as stores, banks, medical facilities?	___ ___	• Interview - student, family • Interview - special educator • Situational assessment • Simulated class activities
10. Does the student participate in the political process (e.g., voting if appropriate age)?	___ ___	• Interview - student, family • Person-Centered Planning
11. Is the student knowledgeable about laws and does the student observe the law?	___ ___	• Interview - student, family • Interview - history and special education teachers • Background review

Personal/Social	Need this? No Yes	Methods to Collect Data
1. Does the student interact with and have support from family members?	___ ___	• Interview - student, family • Interview - work-study coordinator • Interview - career technology teacher • Person-Centered Planning • Situational assessment
2. Does the student have a network of age-appropriate friends?	___ ___	• Interview - student, family • Person-Centered Planning • Observation - classes, lunchtime, extracurricular activities
3. Is the student able to conduct himself or herself appropriately in social situations?	___ ___	• Interview - student, family • Interview - teachers • Situational assessment in school and community
4. Does the student demonstrate an understanding of his or her rights as a person with a disability?	___ ___	• Interview - student, family • Interview - teachers • Person-Centered Planning • Background review - IEP • Observation - general educator

(Continued)

Figure 7.2 (Continued)

Personal/Social	Need this? No Yes	Methods to Collect Data
5. Does the student participate in the IEP planning process (e.g., identify needs and interests, develop postschool goals)?	____ ____	• Interview - student, family • Interview - special educator • Observation - IEP meeting
6. Does the student understand and express his or her needs, strengths, preferences, and interests?	____ ____	• Interview - student, family • Interview - teachers • Person-Centered Planning • Observation - general educator
7. Is the student able to advocate for himself or herself in employment, leisure, and community situations?	____ ____	• Interview - student, family • Interview - teachers • Person-Centered Planning • Situational assessment
8. Does the student need ongoing support from adult service providers?	____ ____	• Interview - student, family • Interview - teachers • Person-Centered Planning • Situational assessment • Observations - IEP meetings, classrooms, employment sites

Independent Living	Need this? No Yes	Methods to Collect Data
1. Is the student aware of how to find independent living quarters?	____ ____	• Interview - student, family • Interview - teachers • Person-Centered Planning • Functional academics

2. Is the student able to purchase and prepare food?	____ ____	• Interview - student, family
		• Interview - teachers
		• Person-Centered Planning
		• Situational assessment in
		  Community
		  Consumer science/food service
		  course

3. Does the student know how to arrange for utility services?	____ ____	• Observation in simulated class activity • Functional academics • Observation of self-determination skills
4. If the student will live in a dorm, does he or she require supports or accommodations to do so?	____ ____	• Interview - student, family • Person-Centered Planning • Background review - IEP • Assistive technology assessment
5. Can the student follow daily routines (e.g., get up in the morning, do dishes, clean)?	____ ____	• Interview - student, family • Interview - teachers • Person-Centered Planning • Situational assessment in home environment

Independent Living	Need this? No Yes	Methods to Collect Data
6. Can the student manage medication if needed?	___ ___	• Interview - student, family
7. Does the student require financial support from an adult agency to live independently?	___ ___	• Interview - student, family • Interview - case manager • Person-Centered Planning • Background review
8. Does the student require support (e.g., budgeting, shopping) from family or an adult service provider to live independently?	___ ___	• Interview - student, family • Person-Centered Planning • Background review - IEP • Adaptive behavior assessment
9. Does the student need accommodations or assistive technology devices to live in an independent living situation?	___ ___	• Interview - student, family • Person-Centered Planning • Situational assessment • Assistive technology assessment • Adaptive behavior assessment
10. Does the student know how to maintain a checking and savings account?	___ ___	• Interview - student, family • Functional academics • Simulated class activity • Situational assessment in community
11. Can the student manage money appropriately for his or her level of income?	___ ___	• Interview - student, family • Functional academics • Situational assessment in community (e.g., mall)
12. Does the student understand and manage his or her health and dental needs?	___ ___	• Interview - student, family • Simulated class activity • Situational assessment in community
13. Does the student know what to do in case of an emergency in the home or in the community?	___ ___	• Interview - student, family • Simulated class activity • Simulated activity in community

What methods will provide the information to answer the assessment questions asked?

Figure 7.2 also identifies methods that can be used to answer the sample assessment questions. Work with the student and the family to identify several assessment activities in which the student will participate during the next few months. These could include situational assessment at a job site, visiting a postsecondary program to obtain information about a certain career major, or completing an interest inventory.

How will the assessment data be collected and used in the IEP process?

Chapter 4 presents information about using the outcomes of the assessment process for IEP planning. It is critical to identify who is responsible for setting up and conducting the assessment activities that have been identified. Assessment data must be collected in a systematic manner and presented in a format that can be used easily by the student, the family, and other team members at the IEP meeting. If assessment data are collected and recorded in a systematic manner, it should be easy for school personnel to complete the Summary of Performance (SOP) that is required in IDEA 2004.

How will transition assessment data be used to complete the SOP document?

As mentioned in Chapter 1, IDEA 2004 requires that an SOP be provided to any student whose eligibility for special education services terminates; this can be due to graduation from high school or exceeding the age for which a free appropriate public education is provided under state law. The SOP must include a summary of the student's academic achievement and functional performance as well as recommendations for how the student will meet his or her postsecondary goals. Appendix A includes a sample completed SOP form for one state. Consult your state department of education or local school district to determine the format that they are using. Chapter 4 presents examples of integrating transition assessment results in the IEP (present level of academic and functional performance). In the same manner, the SOP is an excellent tool for integrating transition assessment results to help the student meet his or her postsecondary goals. Completing such a document will allow the IEP team at the "sending" level to summarize what they know about the student and allow the IEP team at the "receiving" level to determine what additional information needs to be collected, as well as what information needs to be updated. We recommend that the SOP be completed at major transition points for the student (e.g., transition from middle/junior high school to high school) rather than just once as the student exits school. By doing so, the SOP can be completed in a more detailed manner and become part of the transition assessment process. IEP team members can reflect on what they know about the student and what additional information needs to be collected as the student progresses through high school.

SUMMARY

Transition assessment is an ongoing, coordinated, and individualized process.

This chapter included Figure 7.1, which depicts the three components of transition assessment:

1. Identify the student's needs, strengths, preferences, and interests through a variety of assessment methods which are presented in Chapter 6.

2. Identify and analyze current and future living, working, and educational environments to determine the demands of the environment and the resources and supports that may be available. Again, methods to accomplish this are presented in Chapter 6 and Appendices C, D, and E.

3. Use the data to determine the best matches for a student in terms of his or her desired adult roles for independent living, employment, postsecondary education, and/or community involvement. This includes identifying formal and natural supports the student will need to succeed in specific environments, along with accommodations, assistive technology, and interagency resources that are needed to facilitate the match.

This chapter also provided guidelines for developing a plan for transition assessment that is updated over time. In order to individualize the process for each student, a list of potential assessment questions and methods to collect the information was provided in Table 7.2. Finally, it is important that transition assessment data be summarized and used in the IEP process and for the SOP document. Students should also be able to use the data to identify their needs, strengths, preferences, and interests along with postsecondary goals at their yearly IEP meetings. This information can be presented orally, through a one-page written profile, or through a PowerPoint presentation. The IEP team needs to use this information to identify transition services for the student beginning no later than age 16 (we would recommend much earlier) and to complete the SOP document at key points in the student's transition preparation and as the student exits school.

—

Appendix A

Summary for Postsecondary Living, Learning, and Working

Summary for Postsecondary Living, Learning, and Working
(To be completed at exit prior to graduation)

Student Name: José ____   Birthdate: 02-01-87   Date: 03-08-05

Attending District/Building: Anywhere HS ____   Date of Exit: 05-25-05

Postsecondary Expectations:

Living

  Eventually live independently in own home – in an apartment at college

Learning

  BA in architecture – starting at the Not Too Far Away Community College in Fall, 2005

Working

  Work as an architect – do some part-time work while at community college and summers – but not at 4-year college

Recent Special Education Services (Indicate all received within three years prior to exit.)

☐ Behavior Supports   ☐ Communication   ☐ Braille Instruction
☐ Assistive Technology   ☐ Accommodations   ☐ ESL Services
☐ Modifications   ☐ Specially Designed Instruction   ☐ Health
☐ Additional Services (e.g. Speech, Occupational Therapy, Physical Therapy, Transportation)

_____   _____   _____

_____   _____   _____

Goal Areas (Within three years prior to exit)

Reading _____   Written Language _____   Math _____

Self-Determination _____   _____   _____

Describe Student's Current Levels of Performance, as Related to Living, Learning, Working. (Include type of assessment, date of administration, and results.)

Living – José helps out at home – has a checking account and can do most things related to living in an apartment like other people his age. Learning – José made gains in all areas but continues to struggle with spelling, general language and math calculation. He comprehends at grade level with accommodations. Working – José has had several successful summer landscaping jobs and successfully completed a work experience. Employers said he was a hard worker and dependable employee.

Describe Functional Impact of the Disability (as related to Living, Learning, Working)

Living – José's disabilities should have minimal impact on living on his own – in an apartment or home. He will need to use at least a calculator to manage his finances. Learning – José will continue to need to use accommodations in order to get a bachelor's degree. Working – José's difficulties in math will make it difficult for him to be an architect. He will need to learn to accommodate his disability in this area. His work attitudes, ethic, and abilities to work with people will be an asset to him.

Response to Instruction and Accommodations (as Related to Living, Learning, Working)

José's total education program has been provided in the general education setting. He has worked on standards and benchmarks at each grade level and will graduate with a regular diploma. With the use of books on tape he went from 71st percentile to 89th percentile on grade level material in 36 weeks' instruction. With the use of a computer to write and make spelling and grammar checks he went from 30th percentile to 87th percentile, as compared to a progress from the 30th percentile to the 59th percentile without the accommodation. In math José went from the 3rd percentile to the 18th percentile, without a calculator. When allowed to use a calculator his scores went from the 3rd percentile to the 48th percentile.

Recommendations for (Include suggestions for accommodations, linkages to adult services, or other supports.)

Living – Use of calculator, possibly software for personal budget, finances- May need to have prescription and complicated medical information read to him and recorded.

Learning – Books on tape – some auditory accommodation to give content, note takers, computer for writing, calculator. Will need to demonstrate at community college that he can be successful in math coursework. This may be possible in one year, but José may want to consider 2 years at the community college before transferring. He will need to contact the disability support service provider at the 4-year college.

Working – José wants to work part-time while in community college. If he does so, he may want to consider taking less than a full load of coursework. The team recommends that he apply for financial aid so that he will not have to work while taking classes at a 4-year college. José may want to further explore jobs in the same career area as architecture but ones that require less academic training.

Adult/Community Contacts:

Agency: Iowa Vocational Rehabilitation

Status: Picked up application has yet to complete

Name/Position: Ian Summers/rehab counselor

Phone: _____

Agency: Not Too Far Away Community College

Status: met with DSS provider- documentation submitted

Name/Position: <u>Lee T. Mehelp/Disability Support</u>
<u>Services Coordinator</u>   Phone: _____

Agency: _____   Status: _____

Name/Position: _____   Phone: _____

High School Contacts:

Primary High School Contact: Phone: _____
Name/Position: <u>Ila B. Hear</u>

Additional team members contributing to this summary:

Student: <u>José</u>   Parent: <u>Rita</u>

Name/Position: <u>Mrs. Hear/teacher</u>   Name/Position: <u>Lee T. Mehelp/</u>
                                                            <u>NTFA College</u>

Appendix B

*Selected Commercially Available
Tests/Assessment Procedures*

Selected Commercially Available Tests/ Assessment Procedures	Employment	Further Education/Training	Leisure Activities	Daily Living	Community Participation	Health	Self-Determination	Communication	Interpersonal Relationships
Achievement									
Brigance Inventory of Essential Skills	x	x						x	
Hammill Multiability Achievement Test (HAMAT)		x						x	
Iowa Test of Basic Skills (ITBS)		x						x	
Peabody Individual Achievement Test (PIAT)		x						x	
Stanford Achievement Tests-9		x							
Wechsler Individual Achievement Test-2 (WIAT-2)		x						x	
Woodcock-Johnson III (WJIII)		x						x	
Adaptive Behavior									
AAMR Adaptive Behavior Scales-School (ABS-S:2 and ABS-RC:2)	x			x	x			x	x
AAMR Supports Intensity Scale (SIS)	x	x		x	x	x	x		x
Adaptive Behavior Assessment System-2 (ABAS-2)									
Adaptive Behavior Evaluation Scale-H-R	x	x	x	x	x	x	x	x	x
Adaptive Behavior Inventory (ABI)	x	x		x	x			x	x
Inventory for Client and Agency Planning (ICAP)		x	x	x	x			x	x

Selected Commercially Available Tests/ Assessment Procedures	Employment	Further Education/Training	Leisure Activities	Daily Living	Community Participation	Health	Self-Determination	Communication	Interpersonal Relationships
Scales of Independent Behavior, Revised (SIB-R)	x		x	x	x			x	x
Vineland Adaptive Behavior Scales-II (VABS-II)	x			x	x			x	x
Street Survival Skills Questionnaire (SSSQ)				x	x	x			
Aptitude									
Ability Explorer	x	x							
APTICOM	x	x							
Aptitude Interest Inventory	x	x							
Armed Services Vocational Aptitude Battery	x								
Career Ability Placement Survey (CAPS)	x	x							
Career Planning Survey	x								
Employee Aptitude Survey	x								
Explore	x	x							
McCarron-Dial System	x	x							
Occupational Aptitude Survey and Interest Schedule-3 (OASIS-3)	x	x							
Practical Assessment Exploration System (PAES)	x			x					
Talent Assessment Program	x								
Vocational Interest, Temperament, and Aptitude System (VITAS)	x								

(Continued)

(Continued)

Selected Commercially Available Tests/ Assessment Procedures	Employment	Further Education/Training	Leisure Activities	Daily Living	Community Participation	Health	Self-Determination	Communication	Interpersonal Relationships
Cognitive Ability/Learning Aptitude									
Comprehensive Test of Nonverbal Intelligence		x							
Detroit Tests of Learning Aptitude-2		x							
Differential Aptitude Test-5	x	x							
Kaufman Assessment Battery for Children-II		x							
Scholastic Abilities Test for Adults		x							
Stanford-Binet Intelligence Scale-5		x							
Test of Nonverbal Intelligence-3		x							
Wechsler Adult Intelligence Scale-III		x							
Wechsler Intelligence Scale for Children-IV		x							
Wechsler Preschool and Primary Scale of Intelligence-III		x							
Woodcock-Johnson Tests of Cognitive Ability-III		x							
Communication									
Communication Abilities in Daily Living-2 (CADL-2)			x					x	
Comprehensive Receptive and Expressive Vocabulary Test-2 (CREVT-2)								x	

Selected Commercially Available Tests/ Assessment Procedures	Employment	Further Education/Training	Leisure Activities	Daily Living	Community Participation	Health	Self-Determination	Communication	Interpersonal Relationships
Expressive Vocabulary Test (EVT)							x		
Mather-Woodcock Group Writing Test (MWGWT)								x	
Oral and Written Language Scales (OWLS)								x	
Peabody Picture Vocabulary Test (PPVT)								x	
Woodcock Reading Mastery Test (WRMT)								x	
Test of Written Language (TOWL-3)								x	
Functional Capacity									
Ansell-Casey Life Skills Assessment (Level III)	x		x	x	x	x	x	x	x
Comprehensive Adult Student Assessment System (CASAS)	x			x	x	x		x	
Functional Skills Screening Inventory	x	x	x		x			x	x
General Health Questionnaire						x			
Learning Styles									
Barsch Learning Style Inventory	x	x						x	
Piney Mountain Learning Styles Inventory	x	x						x	

(Continued)

(Continued)

Selected Commercially Available Tests/ Assessment Procedures	Employment	Further Education/Training	Leisure Activities	Daily Living	Community Participation	Health	Self-Determination	Communication	Interpersonal Relationships
Manual Dexterity									
Crawford Small Parts Dexterity Test	x								
Peabody Developmental Motor Scales and Activity Cards	x								
Pennsylvania Bi-Manual Dexterity Test	x								
Occupational Interest									
Ashland Interest Assessment (AIA)	x	x							
Career Assessment Inventory (CAI)	x	x							
Career Directions Inventory (CDI)	x	x							
Career Maturity Inventory-Revised (R-CMI)	x	x							
Harrington-O'Shea Career Decision-Making System-Revised	x	x							
Interest Determination Exploration and Assessment System (IDEAS)	x	x							
Minnesota Importance Questionnaire	x	x							
Occupational Aptitude Survey and Interest Scale-3	x	x							
Reading-Free Vocational Interest Inventory-2	x	x							
Self-Directed Search	x	x							
Your Employment Selection (YES)	x	x							

Selected Commercially Available Tests/ Assessment Procedures	Employment	Further Education/Training	Leisure Activities	Daily Living	Community Participation	Health	Self-Determination	Communication	Interpersonal Relationships
Personality/Social Skills									
Adult Personality Inventory, Revised (API-R)	x								x
Behavioral and Emotional Rating Scale									x
Behavior Assessment System for Children									x
Behavior Evaluation Scale-2		x							x
Basic Personality Inventory									x
California Test of Personality									x
Culture-Free Self-Esteem II (Form B)									x
Sixteen Personality Factor (16PF) Questionnaire									x
Social Skills Rating System							x	x	x
Walker-McConnell Scale of Social Competence and School Adjustment							x		x
Prevocational/Employability									
ACCU Vision-Workplace Success Skills	x								
Brigance Employability Skills Inventory	x								
Short Employment Tests-2	x								
Vocational Adaptation Rating Scales	x							x	x
Vocational Integration Index	x								x

(Continued)

Selected Commercially Available Tests/ Assessment Procedures	Employment	Further Education/Training	Leisure Activities	Daily Living	Community Participation	Health	Self-Determination	Communication	Interpersonal Relationships
Wonderlic Basic Skills Test (WBST)									
Work Adjustment Scale	x								x
World of Work Inventory	x								
Transition/Community Adjustment									
Arc's Self-Determination Scale							x	x	x
Brigance Life Skills Inventory				x	x	x		x	
Enderle-Severson Transition Scales (E-STS)	x	x	x	x	x				x
LCCE Knowledge and Performance Battery	x		x	x	x	x			x
Responsibility and Independence Scale for Adolescents	x		x	x	x			x	x
Transition Behavior Scale-2 (TBS-2)	x				x				x
Transition Competence Battery for Deaf Adolescents and Adults	x	x		x	x	x			x
Transition Planning Inventory (TPI)	x	x	x	x	x	x	x	x	x
Quality of Life Questionnaire							x		x
Quality of Student Life Questionnaire							x		x

SOURCE: From *Assessment for Transitions Planning* by Gary M. Clark (2007), pp. 81–85. Copyright 2007 by Pro-Ed. Reprinted with permission.

NOTE: Table content was prepared with the assistance of Gary Bailey, Stelios Gragoudas, Hyo Eun Lee, and Praphal Niduram, graduate students in the Department of Special Education, University of Kansas, Spring 2005.

Appendix C

Community Assessment Form

Dates of Assessment _____   Compiled by _____

City/County/Community _____

The headings in *Community Assessment* are aligned with postsecondary outcomes specified in the definition of transition services from IDEA 2004. In addition, transportation is included to encourage optimal independence for students with disabilities.

STUDENT IDENTIFICATION INFORMATION

Name: _____

Telephone(s): _____

_____

_____

Email: _____

Address : _____

_____

Postsecondary goals:

_____

_____

_____

1. COMMUNITY RESOURCES

(List organizations, services/activities, Web site/telephone)

1A.   Recreational resources

Parks and recreation services

YMCA, gym facilities

Community theatres/arts facilities

Museums, local attractions

Movie theatres

Libraries

Other

1B.   Religious resources (List organizations and services and Web site or telephone)

1C.   **Consumer resources** (List organizations/businesses and services and Web site or telephone)

Medical services

Health services

Social services

Grocery stores, banks

Other

2. SERVICES FOR INDIVIDUALS WITH DISABILITIES

(State and/or local name, services, Web site/telephone, address)

2A.   **Vocational rehabilitation**

2B.   **Developmental disabilities**

2C.   **Mental health services**

2D.   **Social Security benefits office**

2E.   **Local adult service providers (not-for-profit agencies)**

2F.   **Other**

3. EMPLOYMENT RESOURCES

(List organization/business, type of services, contact information, Web site/telephone)

3A.   **Sources for job openings**

One-stop career center

Local newspapers

Web sites for community or state listings

Employment offices

Vocational rehabilitation

Secondary work-study teachers

3B.   **Examples of businesses within a 5-mile radius of the student's home**

3C.   **Community adult service providers**:

Which of the adult service providers (identified in 2E) fund individual job coaching?

Which of the adult service providers (identified in 2E) fund supported employment?

Which of the adult service providers (identified in 2E) fund day habilitation programs?

4. POSTSECONDARY EDUCATION, VOCATIONAL EDUCATION, ADULT AND CONTINUING EDUCATION

Type	Programs/activities	Web site or telephone
4a. Programs or services for students ages 18 to 21 funded by local school systems		
4b. Community college		
4c. Colleges or universities		
4d. Continuing education (local school system)		
4e. Continuing education (community college)		
4f. Public career/ technical schools		
4g. Private career/ technical schools		
4h. Apprenticeship programs		
4i. Other		

5. INDEPENDENT LIVING

(List name of organization that provides residential services in the locale and Web site/ telephone)

5A.   Agencies

Social services

Department of housing

Developmental disabilities

State Medicaid waivers

Other

5B.   Which of the adult service providers (identified in 2E) provide residential options or services to support individuals with disabilities to live independently?

6. TRANSPORTATION INFORMATION

What type of transportation is available to reach employment and community resources? Start your search on the Internet. Using Google, type city, county, or state and special transportation (also try paratransit or specialized transportation for people with disabilities).

Useful Web sites:

6A. Public transportation (attach appropriate information)

(If public transportation is available, please attach appropriate schedule.)

Transportation mode	Yes	No	Web site or telephone	Special fare? Vouchers?
Bus				
Subway				
Light rail				
Special public bus				
Special public van				
Paratransit options (state/county government)				

How does the student access special services and/or fares? _____

_____

_____

6B.   Taxi service

Company	Telephone	Accommodations or special services voucher programs

How does the student access special services and or fares? _____

_____

_____

6C.   Other transportation services (e.g., carpools)

Appendix D

Job Analysis Form

Job Title:

Job Location:

Address:

City:

Phone:

Nature of Business:

Number Employed: Male   Female

Person Interviewed:

Position:

Interviewer:

Date:

Conditions of Interview and Observation

A.   Basic Qualifications

1. Age: _____
    Comments:

2. Experience: None Required   Some Required   Degree
    Comments:

3. Tests: None Given   Given
    Comments:

4. Application: Needed   Not Needed
    Comments:

5. Health Requirements:
   a. Medical Examination: No   Yes   Cost
   b. Specific Tests: No   Yes   Cost

   Comments:

6. Physical Requirements:
   a. Hearing: Exceptional   Average   Not Essential
   b. Eyesight: Exceptional   Average   Not Essential
      1. Color discrimination: Important   Not Important
      2. Spatial discrimination: Important   Not Important
      3. Depth perception: Important   Not Important
   c. Speech: Exceptional   Average   Not Essential
   d. Strength: Exceptional   Average   Not Essential
   e. Endurance: Exceptional   Average   Not Essential

   Comments:

Physical Demand	Much	Little	None
Lift			
Carry			
Push			
Pull			
Walk			
Run			
Climb			
Stoop			
Kneel			
Crouch			
Crawl			
Reach			
Stand			
Sit			
Turn			
Balance			

7. Physical Demands (Check One)

   Comments:

8. Educational Requirements (Circle One)

   No formal education   8th grade completion   College diploma
   Some high school   High school diploma   Master's degree
   Trade/Vocational   Some college

   Comments:

9. Essential Skills (General)

   a. Travel Skills: Local   City   State   None

   Comments:

   b. Telephone Skills: Much Little   None

   Comments:

   c. Customer Relations: Much   Little   None

   Comments:

   d. Supervisor Relations: Much   Little   None

   Comments:

   e. Employee Relations: Much   Little   None

   Comments:

10. Essential Skills (Manual)

    a. Tool Knowledge: Much   Little   None

    Comments:

    b. Machine Knowledge: Much   Little   None

    Comments:

c. Manual Dexterity: Outstanding   Average   Not Important

Comments:

d. Motor Coordination: Outstanding Average Not Important

Comments:

e. Eye-hand-foot coordination: Outstanding Average Not important

Comments:

f. Finger Dexterity: Outstanding   Average   Not Important

Comments:

g. Precision & Accuracy: Outstanding   Average   Not Important

Comments:

11. General Requirements
   a. License: No Yes Type:

   Comments:

   b. Bond: No Yes Type:

   c. Uniform No Yes Type:

   d. Union Membership
       1. Not Available   Available
       2. Not Required   Required
       3. Name of Union
       4. Name of Local   Address
       5. Initial Fee   Dues

   Comments:

B. Working Conditions

   1. Wages
      a. Paid: Hourly Weekly Bimonthly Piecework Monthly

      b. Check   Cash

c. Overtime

d. Holidays

e. Increase: Possible   Impossible

Comments:

2. Hours: More than 40   40   35 or less   Varying

Comments:

3. Days: 6 day week   5 ½ day week   5 day week   Varying

Comments:

4. Length: Year-Round   Seasonal   Permanent   Uncertain

Comments:

5. Benefits:
    a. Vacation: Greater than 2 weeks   One week with/without pay

Comments:

b. Sick Leave: Paid   Not Paid

Comments:

c. Health Insurance: Provided   Not provided

Comments:

d. Dental Insurance: Provided   Not provided

Comments:

e. Retirement: Provided   Not provided

Comments:

f. Workman's Compensation: Provided   Not Provided

Comments:

6.   Hazards

Comments:

7.   Surroundings:

a. Very pleasant   Pleasant   Unpleasant

Comments:

b. Indoors   Outdoors Both

Comments:

c. Noisy   Average   Quiet

Comments:

d. Temperature: Hot   Average   Cold

Comments:

e. Wet   Average   Dry

Comments:

f. Lighting: Well-lit   Adequate   Poorly lit

Comments:

8. Work with: Many others   Some others   Alone

Comments:

9. Supervision:

   a. Much   Some   Little

   Comments:

   b. Sympathetic   Impersonal   Unsympathetic

   Comments:

10. On–the-job training: Provided   Not provided

    Comments:

C. Work Performed

1. On a separate sheet of paper, list all duties and responsibilities observed in the performance of the job. Be specific.

2. On this same separate sheet of paper, list duties and responsibilities not observed. Be specific.

Appendix E

Vocational Training Analysis Form

PART 1: CAREER AND TECHNOLOGY
PROGRAMS OVERVIEW

Before you complete the vocational training analysis, visit the guidance department or identify a person in the school who can assist you in obtaining the following
information:

1. Describe the career and technology programs at this school (vocational-
   technical education, career/technology, tech-prep, school-to-careers). Attach
   a brochure or other program material if available. Have the programs'
   (names and/or content) changed substantially in the past 2 to 3 years?

2. Describe the type of school these programs are offered in: technology
   center, vocational high school, 2 years at high school and then 2 years at
   community college.

3. In what grade(s) do students typically enroll in these programs?

4. How do students in this school system find out about these programs?

5. Do students receive any type of support services while enrolled in these
   programs if they require assistance?

6. Other comments/points of interest:

PART II: ANALYSIS OF VOCATIONAL-TECHNICAL EDUCATION PROGRAM

DATE _____

General Information

Program Name _____

School _____ Instructor _____

Program Length _____

Telephone Number _____ Best Times to Call _____

Program Description

List the major objectives of your program (you can attach a copy of the course syllabus or objectives if available from the instructor).

Do students learn a "code" in your program (e.g., an electrician's or plumber's code) or must they pass a state examination at the end of their training (e.g., cosmetology state board)?

Describe the safety rules and tests that must be followed and passed for entrance into your program.

Prerequisite Skills

Describe the types of prerequisite skills that the instructor would like students to have as they enter the vocational program.

Educational Skills

Math: _____ Adding/Subtracting   _____ Multiplying/Dividing

_____ Fractions   _____ Decimals

_____ Other (Describe.) _____

Reading: Estimated grade level _____

What grade level reading is required for the textbook you use?

_____ Must be able to read study sheets or tests.

_____ Must be able to take notes.

_____ Must be able to write papers.

Describe any modifications the instructor is willing to make.

Behavioral Skills (Check those that are critical.)

_____ Following directions

_____ Coming to class prepared

_____ Working independently

_____ Working in groups

_____ Paying attention

_____ Other (Please list.) _____

Physical Skills (Check those that are critical.)

_____ Walking   _____ Eye-hand coordination
_____ Lifting number of pounds _____   _____ Form perception
_____ Kneeling   _____ Color discrimination
_____ Crouching   _____ Spatial perception
_____ Finger dexterity
_____ Other   (Describe.)   _____

Instructional Methods

Describe the teaching methods you use, including materials (audiovisuals, work-shops, hands-on activities) and structure (small groups, lecture, discussion).

What kinds of assignments do students have to complete in this program (e.g., worksheets, papers, computations, demonstration/laboratory projects)?

Describe the ways students are tested:
_____ Oral
_____ Demonstration
_____ Written tests
_____ Blueprints
_____ Other   (Describe.)   _____

Note any modifications the instructor is willing to make.

What percent of time do students spend in

Classroom with theory?	_____ %
Shop with hands-on activities?	_____ %
The community on class "jobs"?	_____ %
Work experience?	_____ %

Other (Please list comments.) _____

Support Services

What support services are available to students with special needs (students from lower socioeconomic backgrounds or students with disabilities)? Describe any such services, including the availability of vocational support service teams, resource teachers, etc.

Are there any additional support services (or cooperative efforts) that you think are needed for students with special needs to be successful in your program?

_____ No

_____ Yes (Please describe.) _____

What type of jobs do students tend to get after exiting this program? Are there specific postsecondary programs some students transition to?

Is there a person at this school designated to help career and technology students find employment? (If yes, describe.)

In your opinion, is this career and technology instructor willing to work with students with disabilities? Explain. What would you change (in the curriculum, competencies, collaboration strategies) to facilitate students with disabilities in entering and completing this program?

Index

CORWIN PRESS

The Corwin Press logo—a raven striding across an open book—represents the union of courage and learning. Corwin Press is committed to improving education for all learners by publishing books and other professional development resources for those serving the field of PreK–12 education. By providing practical, hands-on materials, Corwin Press continues to carry out the promise of its motto: **"Helping Educators Do Their Work Better."**